HOUSE of WHITE BIRCHES

BIG
Book of
$5.00
Gift
Crafts™

Edited by Laura Scott

HOUSE of
WHITE
BIRCHES

PUBLISHERS
SINCE 1947

Big Book of $5 Gift Crafts

Copyright © 2002 House of White Birches, Berne, Indiana 46711

Editor: Laura Scott

Associate Editor: Cathy Reef

Design Manager: Vicki Blizzard

Technical Editor: Lăna Schurb

Copy Editors: Michelle Beck, Nicki Lehman, Mary Martin

Publication Coordinators: June Sprunger, Tanya Turner

Photography: Tammy Christian, Jeff Chilcote, Kelly Heydinger, Justin P. Wiard

Photography Assistant: Linda Quinlan

Production Coordinator: Brenda Gallmeyer

Graphic Arts Supervisor: Ronda Bechinski

Book/Cover Design: Jessi Butler

Graphic Artist: Amy S. Lin

Production Assistants: Janet Bowers, Marj Morgan

Traffic Coordinator: Sandra Beres

Technical Artist: Chad Summers

Publishers: Carl H. Muselman, Arthur K. Muselman

Chief Executive Officer: John Robinson

Marketing Director: Scott Moss

Book Marketing Manager: Craig Scott

Product Development Director: Vivian Rothe

Publishing Services Manager: Brenda R. Wendling

Printed in the United States of America
First Printing: 2002
Library of Congress Number: 00-112275
ISBN: 1-882138-75-9

A Note
from the
Editor

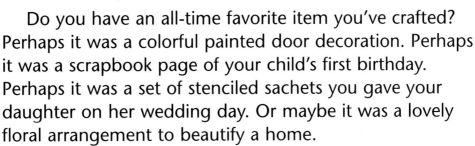

Dear Crafter,

Do you have an all-time favorite item you've crafted? Perhaps it was a colorful painted door decoration. Perhaps it was a scrapbook page of your child's first birthday. Perhaps it was a set of stenciled sachets you gave your daughter on her wedding day. Or maybe it was a lovely floral arrangement to beautify a home.

Whatever your favorite item is, I suspect you gave it away as a special gift for someone you love. Since becoming a craft editor, this is what I've found over and over again—crafters are generous, sharing people who oftentimes give away what they make. I'm sure each and every one of you fits this mold perfectly!

In this book, we've brought you a collection of all-new craft designs that are especially suited to being gift items. To save you money, each item can be made for $5 or less! By using your supplies to make several of each item, you will save money, have an item to give as a gift, and even have a few extra to sell at your next craft fair.

We hope you enjoy this collection. Who knows? Maybe one of these patterns will become your *new* all-time favorite!

Warm regards,

Laura Scott

Contents

1 Friendship Gifts

2 Happy House Warmers

3 Celebrate Love

4 Hugs & Kisses

5 Fun for Kids

7 Merry Christmas

Contents • 5

Friendship Gifts

Spread a little sunshine and cheer with this collection of delightful projects! They're just what you need to lift the spirits of a friend who is sick or shut-in, or simply feeling blue. These crafts are so winsome and sunny, you might just find yourself making them to share with someone you love "just because"!

Floral Candle & Candleholder

Designs by Carolyn V. Stearns

Materials
- 3" x 6" white pillar candle
- Faster Plaster and Faster Plaster candle-holder mold from Plaid
- Rubbing alcohol
- Americana acrylic paints from DecoArt: pineapple #DA6, lemon yellow #DA11, tangerine #DA12, Georgia clay #DA17, baby pink #DA31, baby blue #DA42, desert turquoise #DA44, mistletoe #DA53, bright green #DA54, Indian turquoise #DA87, sapphire blue #DA99, red violet #DA140, blue violet #DA141, blue green #DA142, royal fuchsia #DA151, tangelo #DA196, primary yellow #DA201
- Candle Painting Medium from DecoArt
- Paintbrushes: #1, #3 and #6 rounds and #1 liner

Project Notes
Refer to photo and patterns throughout.

Follow manufacturer's instructions for working with Faster Plaster, candle painting medium and paints.

Let conditioner and paints dry between applications.

Instructions
1. Make candleholder with Faster Plaster as directed by manufacturer; let dry completely.

2. Clean candle with rubbing alcohol.

Mix paints and candle painting medium as directed.

3. Positioning various blossoms randomly over surface, paint flowers onto candle and candleholder: Paint center and petals in colors indicated for specific color combinations that follow. When dry, use indicated color to outline petals, add details to petals, and, using tip of paintbrush handle dipped in paint, dot paint around centers and add a cluster of three dots in center of flower centers.

Orange flowers—tangerine center, tangelo petals, Georgia clay details and dots.

Turquoise flowers—Indian turquoise center, desert turquoise petals, blue green details and dots.

Blue flowers—baby blue center, sapphire blue petals, blue violet details and dots.

Pink flowers—baby pink center, royal fuchsia petals, red violet details and dots.

Yellow flowers—pineapple center, lemon yellow petals, primary yellow details and dots.

4. Add leaves as desired, painting leaves with mistletoe and adding outlines and details with bright green. ❀

Floral Candle Flowers & Leaves

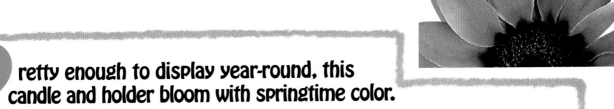

Pretty enough to display year-round, this candle and holder bloom with springtime color.

T
hese long-stem beauties are so much fun, you'll want to make a dozen to share!

Flower Power & Love Bugs Plant Sticks

Design by Carolyn V. Stearns

Materials

- 2 flower plant sticks with ladybugs on springs from Darice
- 2 (3") wooden signs from Lara's Crafts
- 3 half-ladybugs from Darice
- 2 (¼") wooden furniture plugs
- ⅜" checkerboard stencil
- Craft glue
- ZIG .03 black Millennium marker from EK Success Ltd.
- Krylon products: Spray Gesso and Crystal Clear sealer
- Americana acrylic paints from DecoArt: white wash #DA2, baby pink #DA31, desert turquoise #DA44, leaf green #DA51, lamp black #DA67, Indian turquoise #DA87, red violet #DA140, blue green #DA142, royal fuchsia #DA151, Santa red #DA170
- Paintbrushes: #1 and #6 rounds, #0 liner, #8 shader, #2 stencil brush
- Stylus

Project Notes

Refer to photo and patterns throughout.

See directions for base-coating and dry-brushing in "Painting Techniques" in General Instructions on page191.

Let all paints, ink and sealers dry between applications.

Instructions

1. Glue ¼" plug in nose position; spray with gesso.

2. Paint flower center, front and back, referring to following directions for

Continued on page 12

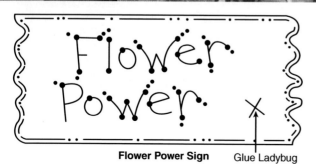

Flower Power Sign   Glue Ladybug here

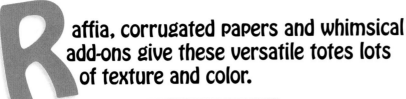

Raffia, corrugated papers and whimsical add-ons give these versatile totes lots of texture and color.

Color Block Gift Totes

Designs by Chris Malone

Materials

All Totes

- Kraft brown bags with handles: 8" x 10" and 2 (4" x 5")
- Paperbilities corrugated papers from MPR: kraft, navy, cranberry and hunter
- Natural raffia
- Embellishments: 3¾" and 1½" rusty tin hearts with holes, 2 plastic red ring beads and 3 plastic blue beads with large holes, 2¾" grapevine star
- Heavy brown paper
- Tapestry needle
- Round hole punch
- Hot-glue gun

Project Note

Refer to photo and pattern throughout.

Tin Hearts Bag

1. Cut rectangles from corrugated paper: *kraft—5" x 4½"; navy—1¼" x 2¾"; cranberry—3⅝" x 1⅞"; hunter—3" x 4¼".* Glue to front of larger bag as shown.

2. Tie raffia bow through holes in larger tin heart; glue to kraft corrugated rectangle.

3. *Note card:* From heavy paper cut 2½" x 5" rectangle; fold in half to make 2½"-square note card. Punch hole in upper left corner. Cut 1⅛" x 1½" rec

tangle cranberry corrugated paper and glue on front of note card; glue smaller tin heart to card so that it overlaps corrugated paper. Tie note card to bag handle with raffia bow.

Small Heart Bag

1. Cut pieces from corrugated paper: *navy—3" x 4" rectangle; cranberry—1⅛" x 1¼" rectangle and heart.*

2. Thread needle with three or four strands of raffia and sew two red beads and one blue bead to center of heart, overlapping beads. Bring all ends of raffia to front of heart and tie in a bow; trim.

3. Glue navy rectangle to bag front; glue red heart with beads to rectangle.

4. *Note card:* From heavy paper, cut 2" x 4" rectangle; fold in half to make 2"-square note card. Punch hole in upper left corner.

Continued on page 18

Rubber stamps make it easy for youngsters to create imaginative, colorful bookmarks for Mom or anyone on their gift lists!

Simple Stamped Bookmark

Design by Beth Wheeler

Materials

- 2" x 6" blank bookmark with tassel from Personal Stamp Exchange
- Black medium-point permanent marking pen
- Rubber stamps in assorted designs
- Metallic gold ink pad (or ink pad in desired color)
- Colored markers

Project Note

Refer to photo throughout.

Instructions

1. Write name or message in center of bookmark with marking pen.

2. Add stamped designs as desired. When ink is dry, color designs with markers. ✿

Flower Power & Love Bugs Plant Sticks continued from page 10

individual designs. Paint petals, front and back; highlight petals. Paint lines down center of petals and dots around center.

Love Bugs—Paint flower center Indian turquoise; paint petals desert turquoise; highlight petals with Indian turquoise; paint petal lines and center dots blue green.

Flower Power—Paint flower center baby pink; paint petals royal fuchsia; highlight petals with baby pink; paint petal lines and center dots red violet.

3. Dry-brush cheeks with royal fuchsia. Paint eyes with white wash; dot on lamp black pupils, and when dry, add tiny white wash highlight dots with

tip of stylus. Paint mouth with lamp black and add a white wash comma stroke highlight to open mouth.

4. Paint ladybug on spring Santa red; add lamp black head, line down back and dots on wings.

5. Base-coat sign as directed in following instructions. When dry, place stencil on surface and stencil every other square with white wash. Add lettering and hearts. Using black marking pen throughout, outline sign lightly; add light squiggly lines around petals. Glue one or two ladybugs to sign.

Love Bugs—Paint sign Indian turquoise; paint letters blue green; paint

hearts (including "O" in "Love") blue green and desert turquoise.

Flower Power—Paint sign baby pink; paint letters red violet.

6. Paint stick leaf green. Glue sign to stick 2" below flower.

7. Spray all surfaces with two or three light coats of sealer. ✿

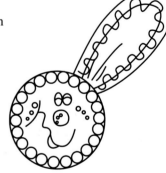

Flower

Glue Ladybug here

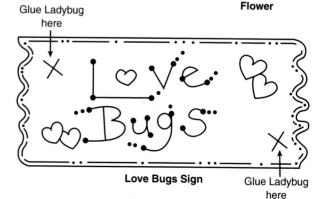

Love Bugs Sign

Glue Ladybug here

A sweet frog, a ladybug and busy bee come to life as fanciful lapel pins.

Garden Critter Pins

Designs by Paula Bales

Materials

Each Pin

- Paintbrushes: #4 shader and 5/0 spotter
- ZIG .05 black Millennium marker from EK Success Ltd.
- 1" pin back
- Tacky glue or hot-glue gun

Frog

- Woodsies circles from Forster: 2 small, 2 medium and 1 large
- Apple Barrel acrylic paints from Plaid: spring green, yellow, bright red, white and black

Ladybug

- Woodsies from Forster: 1 medium circle and 1 large circle
- Apple Barrel acrylic paints from Plaid: bright red, white and black
- 8½" piece Toner Plastics licorice 24-gauge Fun Wire
- Wire cutters

Bee

- Woodsies from Forster: 1 medium circle, 1 large circle and 2 medium eggs
- Apple Barrel acrylic paints from Plaid: yellow, bright red, white and black
- 2½" piece Toner Plastics licorice 24-gauge Fun Wire
- Wire cutters

Project Notes

Refer to photos throughout.

Paint all surfaces of wooden pieces.

Let paints and ink dry between applications.

Frog

1. *Eyes:* Paint small circles white. Add black dots for pupils, positioning them near edge. Add tiny white highlight specks to black pupils. Outline and draw eyes with marker.

2. *Head:* Paint large circle spring green. Add tiny yellow dots; overlapping each, add a tiny white dot. Dot on a bright red nose and tongue. Using marker, outline head and draw mouth.

3. *Legs:* Paint medium circles spring green. Add white stripes and tiny yellow dots between the stripes. Using marker, outline legs and add other details.

4. Glue eyes to top front of head and edges of legs to wrong side of head as shown. Glue pin back to back of frog.

Ladybug

1. *Head:* Paint medium circle black; dot on white eyes; using liner, add white eyebrows and vertical mouth line. Dot tiny black pupils onto eyes; dot on bright red nose.

2. *Body:* Paint large circle bright red. Using pen, draw wing lines and outline body. Dot wings with black and add tiny specks of white. In area between wings, use liner to add white horizontal lines; underscore each white line with marker.

3. *Antennae:* Cut 2½"

piece of wire; bend in half and curl ends. Glue antennae to back of head.

4. *Legs:* Cut six 1" pieces of wire; curl one end of each. Glue straight ends to back of body, three on each side.

5. Glue head to front edge of body; glue pin back to back of body.

Bee

1. *Head:* Paint medium circle black; dot on white eyes and mouth; using liner, add white eyebrows. Dot tiny black pupils onto eyes; dot on bright red nose.

2. *Body:* Paint large circle yellow with three black horizontal stripes. Using liner, add white vertical lines. Using marker, outline body, line each white line and add specks between vertical lines.

3. *Wings:* Paint eggs white. Using liner, add five vertical yellow lines to each (from point to base). Using marker, outline wings and line yellow lines.

4. *Antennae:* Bend wire in half and curl ends. Glue antennae to back of head.

5. Glue head to front edge of body; glue wings to back of body, points touching; glue pin back to back of body. ✾

Buggy Buddies

Designs by Missy Becker

Materials

Ant

- Wooden products: 2 (1") ball knobs, 1⁵⁄₁₆" robin egg, ¼" furniture plug
- 15" piece black wire
- 1½" straw hat
- 2 (4mm) black beads
- 8" piece raffia
- Americana acrylic paints from DecoArt: titanium white #DA1, sand #DA4, lamp black #DA67, honey brown #DA163, peony pink #DA215
- Paintbrushes: #8 shader, #5 round, #0 liner

Ladybug

- Wooden products: 2 (¾") ball knobs, 1⁵⁄₁₆" robin egg, 1½" heart cutout
- 12" piece 24-gauge black wire
- 1½" straw hat
- Scrap of twisted paper or ribbon
- 6"–8" piece raffia
- Americana acrylic paints from DecoArt: titanium white #DA1, sand #DA4, lamp black #DA67, honey brown #DA163, alizarin crimson #DA179, peony pink #DA215
- Paintbrushes: #10 shader, #3 round, #0 liner
- Pencil with unused eraser

Both Projects

- Sup-R Sander from Midwest Products
- Old toothbrush
- Cotton-tip swab
- Toothpick
- Tacky craft glue
- Paper towel

Project Notes

Refer to photo and patterns throughout.

Let paints dry between applications.

Ant

Painting

1. Sand bottom of the egg (tail section) flat. For body, sand one of the ball knobs flat on one side; the other knob—the head—will be positioned here.

2. Using shader brush, paint egg and both ball knobs black.

3. Using round brush and sand paint throughout, paint facial area on head and paint plug (nose).

4. Lightly spatter all painted pieces with old toothbrush and white paint.

5. Float a shadow of honey brown around face. Dip cotton-tip swab into peony pink; rub off most of paint onto a paper towel. Using nearly dry swab, "scrub" cheeks in a circular motion and float bottom edge of nose.

6. Using toothpick or brush handle, dot on black eyes. Thin a little black paint to an inky consistency with water and line eyebrows and mouth with mixture. Lightly spatter face and nose with thinned paint and toothbrush.

7. Using toothpick, dot white highlights onto nose and cheeks.

Assembly

1. Cut wire into three 4" pieces and one 3" piece; set aside 3" piece for now. Form 4" pieces of wire into legs. Glue two to the flat bottom of the egg; glue one to the flat side of head. Glue on body with sanded side facing up. Glue head to flattened side; glue nose to face.

2. Bend 3" piece of wire in half; poke through straw hat. (Use a toothpick as needed to help push the wire through.) Thread beads on ends of wire and twist wire to hold them in place. Glue hat onto ant's head. Tie raffia around its neck; tie in a bow in front.

Ladybug

Painting

1. Sand bottom and one side (back) of the egg flat. Sand one of the ball knobs—the body—flat on one side; other knob—the head—will be positioned here.

2. Using shader, paint egg and both ball knobs black; paint heart (wings) honey brown.

3. Using round brush and sand paint, paint facial area on head.

4. Using shader through step 5, paint heart again with alizarin crimson.

Continued on page 25

All dressed up in straw hats and bows, this wee pair will worm their way into your affections!

*T*his friendly fellow has found a lovely spot to linger among your plants. He's a charming character long after the plant is gone.

Pokey Turtle Plant Poke

Design by Reba Campbell

Materials
- Arch mini garden sign #11242 from Walnut Hollow
- Woodsies 1½" oval from Forster
- Other wooden products: 2½" half-egg, 2 (1") furniture plugs, ½" furniture plug
- Americana acrylic paints from DecoArt: white wash #DA2, mistletoe #DA53, lamp black #DA67, true red #DA129, reindeer moss green #DA187
- ZIG .03 pure black Millennium marker from EK Success Ltd.
- Paintbrushes: ¾", ½" and stencil brush
- Thick craft glue
- ¾" checkerboard stencil
- Toothpick
- Masking tape
- Clear matte sealer

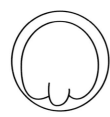

Project Notes
Refer to photo and patterns throughout.

Let all paints, ink and sealer dry between applications.

Use masking tape as needed to hold wooden pieces in place while painting.

Pokey Turtle Face

Pokey Turtle Foot

Instructions
1. Glue oval to wrong side of garden sign (turtle shell) so about half of it protrudes from behind the lower right corner; this will be the turtle's tail. Paint all surfaces of shell, stake and tail mistletoe.

2. Glue ½" button plug (nose) to half-egg (head). Paint head and nose reindeer moss green; paint 1" button plugs (feet) mistletoe.

3. Place stencil over turtle shell; stencil alternating squares with reindeer moss green.

4. Thin a little true red with water; paint cheeks and shade top of nose with mixture. Paint eyes with white wash; paint eyelids mistletoe. Using end of paintbrush, dot on eyes with lamp black. Using toothpick, dot cheeks with white wash.

5. Add details with black marker.

6. Glue head and feet button plugs to front of shell.

7. Spray plant poke with clear matte sealer. ❧

Gardener's Glove Gifts

Designs by Marilyn Gossett

Materials

Ladybug Pin & Notepad Holder

- Wavy corrugated kraft cardboard: 5" x 8" and 3½" x 8½"
- 5" x 8" piece ivory card stock
- Woodsies wooden circles from Forster: 1¼" and ¾"
- Raffia: natural and green
- Ceramcoat acrylic paints from Delta: white #2505, black #2506, opaque red #2507
- Nostalgia corner edgers from Fiskars
- ¾" piece ½"-wide hook-and-loop tape
- 3" square self-adhesive notes

Bumblebee Pin

- 5" x 8" piece ivory card stock
- 1¼" flat wooden heart cutout
- Natural raffia
- Flowers: 1" pink parchment rose, 3 (1") sprigs silk baby's breath, ¼" pink ribbon rose
- Ceramcoat acrylic paints from Delta: white #2505, black #2506, opaque yellow #2509

Each Project

- ⅛" round hole punch
- Black ultra-fine-point marking pen
- Clear craft varnish
- Glue stick
- Tacky craft glue
- 1" pin back
- Clear Dimensional Magic from Plaid
- Paintbrushes: #12 shader, #0 detail liner
- Stylus or toothpick

Project Notes

Refer to photo and patterns throughout.

Let paints, varnish and ink dry between applications.

Follow manufacturer's instructions for using Dimensional Magic. Any warping that occurs when it is applied should correct itself as the piece dries.

Ladybug Pin & Glove

1. *Glove card:* Cut one glove from ivory card stock. Using marking pen, outline glove and add details. (On sample, lettering is omitted; include it if you wish.) Using glove as a template, cut another glove from 5" x 8" kraft cardboard, cutting it ¼" larger all around. Glue card stock glove to cardboard glove. Punch two holes through cuff and two through glove where indicated.

2. *Pin:* Paint all surfaces of 1¼" wooden circle opaque red. Using black throughout, paint head and add line down center; dot ladybug's wings with brush handle dipped in paint. For eyes, apply tiny dots of white to head; when dry, add tiny black pupils with marking pen. Seal all surfaces of pin with varnish.

3. Apply a thin coat of Dimensional Magic to right side of ladybug; let dry completely. Glue pin back to back of pin.

4. Pin ladybug to glove through holes in glove. Thread strands of natural and green raffia through holes on cuff and knot on front of glove; trim ends.

Sweet and simple, these cute, creative pins and note holder borrow popular motifs from nature.

Ladybug Notepad Holder

1. Lay 3½" x 8½" piece wavy corrugated cardboard wavy side down; fold up bottom short edge 1½" and fold down top short edge 3½". Check fit of notepad. Glue hook portion of hook-and-loop tape to center of bottom flap. Fold top down over bottom and glue loop portion to wrong side so pieces of hook-and-loop tape line up. Trim corners of top flap with corner paper edgers.

2. Repeat steps 2 and 3 for pin using ¾" circle, but do not attach pin back.

3. Tie a knot in the middle of a 3½" piece of green raffia; shred ends with your fingers. Glue to center of cover; glue ladybug over raffia knot.

4. Insert pad of notes in holder.

Bee Pin & Glove

1. *Glove card:* Cut one glove from ivory card stock. Using marking pen, outline glove and add details, including lettering if desired. Punch two holes through cuff and two through glove where indicated.

2. *Pin:* Paint all surfaces of wooden heart, painting wings white and body black. When dry, use liner brush to paint four yellow stripes across body. For eyes, apply tiny dots of white to head. Mix equal parts black and white paint; using liner, windowpane wing area and shade edges of wings with mixture. Draw detail on wings and outline stripes with marking pen. Seal all surfaces of pin with varnish.

3. Apply a thin coat of Dimensional Magic to right side of bee; let dry completely. Glue pin back to back of bee.

4. Pin bee pin to glove through holes in glove. Thread strands of raffia through holes on cuff and knot on front of glove. Glue baby's breath, then ribbon and parchment flowers over knot. ❀

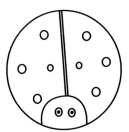

Notepad Holder

Ladybug Pin

Bee Pin

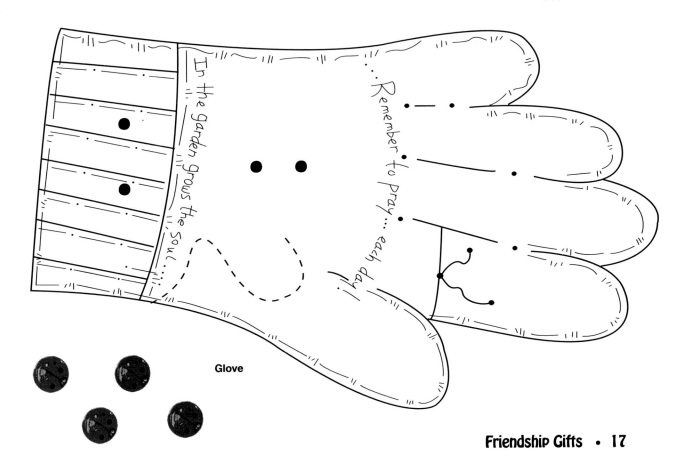

Glove

Ladybug Love Votive Candle

Design by Vicki Blizzard

Materials

- Round clear glass votive candle cup
- 12" square white adhesive vinyl
- Paper Shaper Punch circle paper punches from EK Success Ltd.: ⅜" #PSP01C and ¼" #PSP02C
- Small jar Etchall etching dip from B&B Products
- Rubber stamps from Craft Stamps: ladybug #1029PB, swirl/dots #1023AC and swirly heart #2052TC
- Color Box Cat's Eye Pigment Brush pads from Clearsnap Inc.: cranberry, green and black
- Clear embossing powder #05 from Tsukineko
- Gold Cerne Relief Outliner #773 from Pebeo
- Pepper red #82 Vitrea 160 glossy glass/ceramic felt-tip pen from Pebeo
- Heat embossing tool
- Baking sheet
- Oven

Friendly ladybugs crawl across the surface of this delicately frosted votive candle.

Project Notes

Refer to photo throughout. Follow manufacturers' instructions for using etching dip, embossing powder and vitrea marker.

Instructions

1. Using both paper punches, punch several circles from adhesive vinyl. Peel off adhesive backing and randomly apply to outside of glass votive cup.

2. Following manufacturer's instructions, submerge candle cup in etching dip. Remove from dip; rinse thoroughly and dry. Remove adhesive vinyl circles.

3. Using black pigment brush pad, randomly stamp ladybugs onto outside of candle cup. Immediately pour embossing powder over stamped images. Tap off excess. Melt powder using heat embossing tool.

4. Repeat step 3 using swirl/dots stamp with green pigment brush pad and swirly heart stamp with cranberry pigment brush pad.

5. Using red pepper vitrea marker, color in ladybug bodies.

6. Outline circles with gold relief outliner. Allow to dry thoroughly before baking according to manufacturer's instructions. ❀

Color Blocks Gift Totes continued from page 11

Glue corrugated cranberry rectangle to front of note card. Tie note card to bag handle with raffia bow. Thread a blue bead onto each end of raffia and knot to hold beads in place.

Grapevine Star Bag

1. From kraft corrugated paper, cut 1⅜" square and 3¼" x 4¼" rectangle.

2. Thread needle with raffia and sew star to corrugated rectangle by making five stitches over edges of star. Bring all ends of raffia to front of paper close to star and tie ends in a bow; trim ends.

3. Glue kraft rectangle to bag front.

4. *Note card:* From heavy paper, cut 2" x 4" rectangle; fold in half to make 2"-square note card. Punch hole in upper left corner. Glue corrugated kraft square to front of note card. Tie note card to bag handle with a raffia bow. ❀

Heart

Choose your color scheme and craft a colorful pillow to dress up the décor!

Folk Art Pillow

Design by Kathy Wegner

Materials
- 12" square pillow form
- 2 (15") squares Warm & Natural needled cotton batting from The Warm Company
- Hand-sewing needle
- Straight pins

Muted Colors
- Kunin Rainbow Felt Classic: deep rose #0H2, leaf green #495, wedgewood blue #686
- Ecru 6-strand embroidery floss
- Ivory ¾"–⅞" button

Bright Colors
- Kunin Rainbow Felt Classic: pink punch #0G9, lime #494, blueberry bash #6J2
- Black 6-strand embroidery floss
- Black ¾"–⅞" button

Project Notes
Refer to photo and patterns throughout.

One side of sample pillow was completed using muted colors and the other was completed using bright colors. Complete your pillow as desired.

Instructions
1. Cut pieces for each side of pillow, choosing muted or bright color scheme: four hearts from deep rose or pink punch; one flower from wedgewood blue or blueberry bash; four leaf pairs from leaf green or lime.

2. Using 6 strands embroidery floss, blanket-stitch felt pieces to batting square; attach button to center of flower. Repeat on second batting square if desired.

3. Pin batting squares together, right sides out, sandwiching pillow form between them. Using 6 strands embroidery floss, sew squares together with running stitch, securing pillow form in place. Trim edges of batting evenly ½" from stitching. ❀

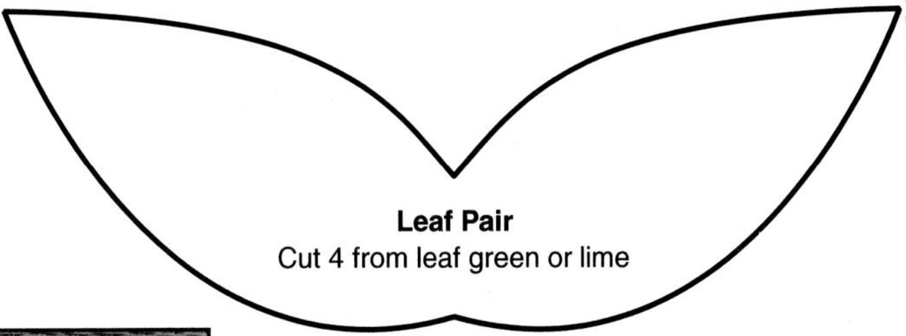

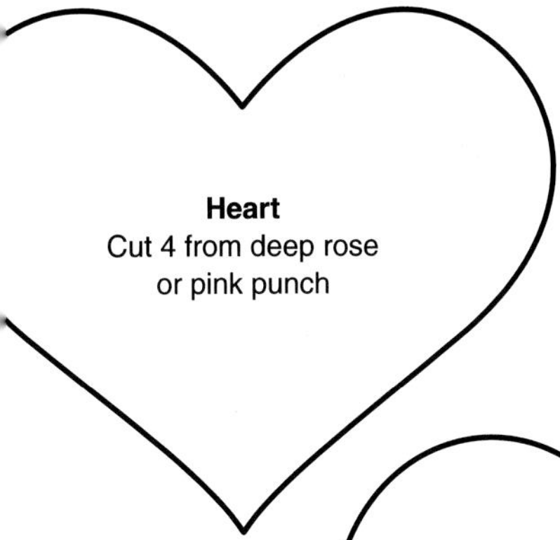

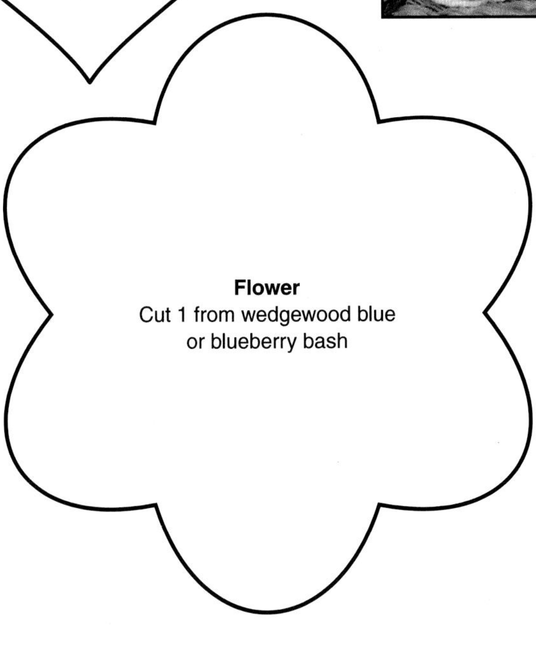

Melon Fizz Gel Candle

Design by Vicki Blizzard

Materials
- 5 ounces each clear and peridot Gel Candle by Delta
- 10" wick by Delta
- Scent by Delta (optional)
- Drinking glass with beaded bottom, approximately 3¾" tall by 3" in diameter
- Glass pie plate
- Fork
- Pencil or wooden skewer
- 2 heavy saucepans

Project Note
Refer to photo throughout.

Instructions
1. Following manufacturer's instructions, melt both colors of gel in separate heavy saucepans. If desired, after removing gel from stove, add scent to melted gel.

2. Dip metal bottom of wick into clear gel and press into center of bottom of glass. Pour peridot gel in bottom of glass to a depth of ¼".

3. Pour remaining peridot gel in a glass pie plate or baking dish. Immediately start whipping gel with fork until it begins to form a ball. Remove ball from dish and start rolling it between the palms of your hands. *Note: Gel is very warm to start, but cools quickly. Continue rolling gel into a ball shape until it is very cool and holds a ball shape when placed on a table. Press wick up through center of cooled ball.*

4. Place ball in glass on top of peridot gel layer, metal end of wick down.

5. Wrap wick around pencil or skewer to hold it centered at top of glass. Pour clear gel into glass to approximately ½" from top. Let gel cool completely and trim wick to ¼" before burning. ❀

This candle resembles a refreshing fizzy drink on a hot summer day!

Sparkly beads glitter and shine in the glow of this candle's flame!

Rainbow Candle

Design by Vicki Blizzard

Materials
- 4 ounces clear Gel Candle by Delta
- 10" wick by Delta
- Scent by Delta (optional)
- Recycled glass jar approximately 5" tall by 2½" in diameter
- 2 large handfuls transparent pony beads
- 24" 20-gauge gold craft wire
- Wire cutters
- ¼" wooden dowel
- Pencil or wooden skewer
- Heavy saucepan

Project Note
Refer to photo throughout.

Instructions
Note: Set aside 16–20 beads to be used when decorating jar.

1. Following manufacturer's instructions, melt gel in a heavy saucepan. If desired, after removing gel from stove, add scent to melted gel.

2. Dip metal bottom of wick into clear gel and press into center of bottom of jar.

3. Holding wick out of the way, pour a small amount of gel down inside of jar, rotating to cover. Quickly add a small amount of beads and allow to cool in gel. Repeat until beads cover sides of jar. Wrap wick around pencil or skewer at top of jar to hold it centered. Fill jar with remaining clear gel and let cool. Trim wick to ¼" before burning.

4. Wrap wire around dowel to form coils every 2". Thread beads onto coils; wrap wire around neck of jar and twist ends. Coil ends of wire and thread beads onto coils. Wrap end of each wire around wire at neck of jar to form two beaded loops. ❀

Country Charm Notepad Holders

Designs by Sandra Graham Smith

Materials

Each Holder

- Repositionable notes: 3" square or 2" x 3"
- Wallpaper scrap
- Colored corrugated board
- Decorative paper edgers
- Brass charm or decorative metallic button
- Tacky craft glue
- Round hole punch
- Natural or colored raffia
- Plastic bag: 4" x 5" or 3" x 4½"

Transform wallpaper scraps and other odds and ends into great little gifts.

Project Notes

Refer to photo and patterns throughout, choosing appropriate patterns for the larger (3" square) or smaller (2" x 3") repositionable notes.

If using a shank button, clip or snap it off before gluing it in place.

Cut pieces with plain scissors unless otherwise instructed.

Instructions

1. Trace pattern for desired cover onto wrong side of corrugated board; cut out. Score dashed line(s) in center on wrong side of corrugated board using straight edge and the point of scissors.

2. Glue pad of notes to back inside cover.

3. Using paper edgers, cut a 1½" square of wallpaper; glue in bottom right corner on front of cover and glue charm or button on top of it.

4. Trace pattern for top onto wrong side of matching wallpaper; cut out, trimming bottom edges with paper edgers.

5. Insert covered notepad into plastic bag; place top over open edge of bag.

6. Punch two holes through top and plastic bag. String raffia through holes and tie in bow on front of bag. ❀

Large Top
4½" x 4" for 3"-square notes
Cut 1 from wallpaper

Large Cover
3½" x 7" for 3"-square notes
Cut 1 from corrugated board

Small Cover
3½" x 5" for 2" x 3" notes
Cut 1 from corrugated board

Small Top
3½" x 3" for 2" x 3" notes
Cut 1 from wallpaper

Patchwork Needle Book & Pincushion

Designs by Samantha McNesby

Materials

Needle Book

- Assorted small fabric scraps in complementary colors/patterns
- Lining fabric at least 5" x 9"
- 2 pieces cotton batting at least 5" x 9"
- A "fat quarter" or large fabric scrap for binding (see Project Notes)
- Small gold heart charm
- ½ yard ⅛" ribbon in complementary colors
- White sewing thread and/or quilting thread
- Hand-sewing and tapestry needles
- Sewing machine (optional)

Pincushion

- Assorted small fabric scraps in complementary colors/patterns
- Backing fabric at least 6" square
- Small amount of stuffing
- White sewing thread and/or quilting thread
- Hand-sewing needle

Project Notes

Refer to photo and pattern throughout.

A "fat quarter" is a quarter-yard of fabric cut 22½" x 18 " rather than 45" x 9". All seam allowances are ¼".

Needle Book

1. *Nine-Patch block:* Cut nine 1½" squares from assorted small fabric scraps. Lay squares out in three rows of three to make a square block. Seam the squares together in each row, then seam the rows together to make Nine-Patch block. Press seams.

2. *Border:* Cut four 4" x 1" strips. Right sides facing, sew one strip across top of Nine-Patch block and another across bottom; then sew border strips up sides, trimming as needed for a good fit.

3. *Back of book:* Cut 4½" square of fabric for back of book (or size to match front). Right sides facing, sew to one of border strips; seam will be spine of book.

4. *Layers:* Cut 5" x 9" lining fabric and batting. Lay lining fabric right side down on work surface. Top with batting; smooth it as needed. Place pieced needle book cover on top, right side up. Pin together layers; quilt as desired.

5. *Binding:* Cut four strips 1½" x 10". Fold under one long edge ¼"; press. Repeat down other side of strip. Lay strip over one short edge of needle book; sew in place with invisible stitches. Repeat with other strips to bind remaining short side, and then long sides. When binding long sides, turn under ends of binding strips and stitch for a neat finish.

6. *Finishing:* Fold book in half; press. Open book and lay flat. From remaining batting cut one piece 3" x 6". Using tapestry needle and thread, attach batting along inside center of needle book along fold, stitching through all thicknesses. Fold book in half. Thread tapestry needle with ribbon. At fold, measure in 1" from edge and take ribbon down through all thicknesses; bring it back to outside of book 1" from other side. Tie ribbon ends in a bow. Stitch charm to front center of needle book.

Pincushion

1. *Pieced top:* Cut a variety of odd shapes from

Dive into your scrap bag for the fabrics for these quaint and sweet sewer's helpers.

assorted small fabric scraps. Lay out shapes on work surface and sew two scraps together. Trim one side of joined pieces; add a third. Continue adding pieces and trimming until you have a 6" square.

2. Lay heart template over pieced fabric; trace and cut out. Cut identical heart shape from backing fabric.

3. Lay backing fabric face-down on work surface. Center pieced heart face up on top, matching edges. Pin together. Sew around ¼" from cut edges, leaving a small opening for stuffing. Stuff heart; sew opening closed. ❀

Heart Pincushion
Cut 1 from pieced fabric for
front and 1 from backing fabric

Buggy Buddies continued from page 14

5. Add shadow to face and create nose by floating or shading with honey brown.

6. Using eraser dipped in black, dot spots onto heart.

7. Using round brush and white paint, add whites of eyes and comma stroke to wings. Lightly spatter all painted pieces with tooth-brush and white paint.

8. Dip cotton-tip swab into peony pink; rub off most of paint onto a paper towel. Using nearly dry swab, "scrub" cheeks in a circular motion.

9. Using black paint and round brush, add pupils to eyes. Float shading on heart with black. Thin a little black paint to an inky

consistency with water; using liner brush, line on eyelashes and mouth.

10. Using toothpick, dot white highlights onto eyes and cheeks.

Assembly

1. Cut wire into four 3" pieces. Bend three of the four wires in half to make the legs and the arm. Glue two to the flat end of the egg, making sure that flat side of egg is facing up and the legs are down. Glue on the body, making sure the flat side is facing up and is in line with the flat side of the egg. There should now be two wires—four legs— between the egg and the knob. Glue the third wire

to the flat side of the body; glue head in place. (Position head so that it is looking to one side, or facing for-ward.) Glue wings to flat side of egg. Let glue dry thoroughly.

2. Bend wires to make feet and hands. Play with legs as needed so that ladybug will stand.

3. Cut straw hat in half. Push last piece of wire through hat to make antennae. (Use a toothpick as needed to help push the wire through.) Glue hat onto head.

4. Find center of raffia; using a small amount of glue, glue it to center of hat behind brim. Pull it around hat and tie under chin. Add

a little glue to back of raffia bow and glue in place at chin. Add a bow of twisted paper to front of hat. ❀

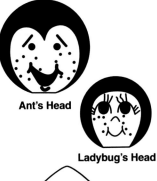

Ant's Head

Ladybug's Head

Ladybug's Wings

Incredible Shrinking Jewelry

Designs by Samantha McNesby

Ever used shrink plastic before? Get out your markers and paints and have a ball!

Materials

Both Pins

- 1 sheet of shrink plastic
- Sharpie medium-point black permanent marker
- Acrylic paints: bright pink, bright blue, turquoise, yellow, orange, bright green, brown
- Small paintbrush
- 2 pin backs
- Thick craft glue or hot-glue gun

Project Notes

Refer to photo and patterns throughout.

Refer to manufacturer's instructions for using and shrinking plastic.

Apply very light coats of paint; colors will darken considerably when baked.

Instructions

1. Trace designs onto shrink plastic using marking pen and leaving at least ¾" between drawings.

2. Paint plastic pieces as shown, mixing yellow and bright green paints to achieve a lighter shade as desired. Let paints dry completely, then cut out, cutting ¼" beyond outlines.

3. Bake pieces according to manufacturer's instructions. Let plastic cool completely before handling.

4. Glue a smaller flower to each section of topiary pin. Glue a pin back to back of each pin. Let glue cure for 24 hours before wearing. ❀

Topiary

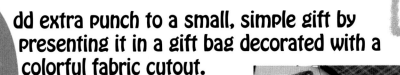

dd extra punch to a small, simple gift by presenting it in a gift bag decorated with a colorful fabric cutout.

Gift Bags

Design by Ann Butler

Materials
Each Gift Bag
- 10½" x 7½" piece twill fabric
- Coordinating fabric of your choice for cutout
- Coordinating sewing threads
- HeatnBond Lite fusible adhesive from Therm O Web
- 22" piece natural jute twine
- 2 coordinating pony beads
- Sewing machine

Project Notes
Refer to photo throughout.

Follow manufacturer's instructions for using fusible adhesive.

Use ⅜"–½" seam allowance throughout.

Instructions
1. Hem 10½" edge of twill fabric. Fold fabric right sides facing; seam raw edges. Turn right side out.

2. Fuse adhesive to wrong side of coordinating fabric; cut out desired motif and fuse to bag.

3. String beads onto twine, one at each end, and knot twine to hold beads in place. Place gift in bag and tie shut with twine. ❀

Small Flowers

Hearts and Flowers

"Home Tweet Home" Canister

Design by Bev Shenefield

Materials

- 4"-diameter terra-cotta flowerpot with saucer
- 1" wooden ball knob
- Sponge
- Industrial-strength craft cement
- Ceramcoat acrylic paints from Delta: Seminole green #2009, apple green #2065, dark chocolate #2021, adobe red #2046, black green #2116, sweetheart blush #2130, liberty blue #2416, rain forest green #2462, hunter green #2471, white #2505, black #2506
- Ceramcoat products from Delta: gesso and exterior gloss varnish
- Paintbrushes: #8 flat, #1 liner, #¾ filbert
- Fine-tip black permanent marker
- .05mm black Micron Pigma pen
- Sandpaper
- Tack cloth
- Toothpick

Project Notes

Refer to photos and pattern throughout. Paint all surfaces of flowerpot, saucer and knob.

Refer to instructions for shading and highlighting under "Painting Techniques" in General Instructions on page 191.

Let all coats of cement, gesso, paint and varnish dry between applications.

Dot on birdhouse openings with tip of paintbrush handle dipped in paint; using same method, dot on perches with toothpick.

Surface Preparation

1. Sand knob, flowerpot and saucer; wipe off dust with tack cloth. Cement knob to center bottom of saucer.

2. Coat all surfaces with gesso. Sponge with liberty blue and white.

3. Trace pattern onto sides of flowerpot.

Painting

1. Paint walls of Birdie Condo apple green; shade with hunter green. Paint roof and post hunter green; highlight roof with apple green. Dot on openings with hunter green; dot on perches with black green. Paint sign white; paint chimney adobe red.

This cute little canister mimics the look of old-fashioned blue graniteware. No one will guess it started out as an inexpensive flowerpot!

2. Paint "For Wrent Cheep" sign and stake with white.

3. Paint walls of round birdhouse adobe red; shade with a mixture of sweetheart blush and adobe red. Paint roof and stake sweetheart blush; highlight roof with adobe red. Dot on opening with chocolate brown and perch with black.

4. Paint walls of Fly Inn Seminole green; shade with mixture of Seminole green and black green. Paint roof and post apple green; shade shingles and post with Seminole green. Dot on openings and perches with black green; paint sign white.

5. Paint walls and post of two-hole birdhouse adobe red. Paint roof and shade walls and post with dark chocolate. Dot on openings with dark chocolate and perches with black.

6. Paint "Vacant Gone South" sign and post with white.

7. Paint walls of three-hole birdhouse and stake with sweetheart blush; shade with dark chocolate and highlight with adobe red. Paint roof adobe red. Dot on openings with dark chocolate and perches with black.

Finishing

1. Outline signs and rim of pot with fine-tip pen. Use .05mm pen to print words on signs and outline birdhouses.

2. Using liner brush and white, print "HOME TWEET HOME" on rim of flowerpot; add dots to ends of lines in letters with tip of paintbrush handle.

3. Seal pot and saucer with at least two coats of gloss exterior varnish. ❀

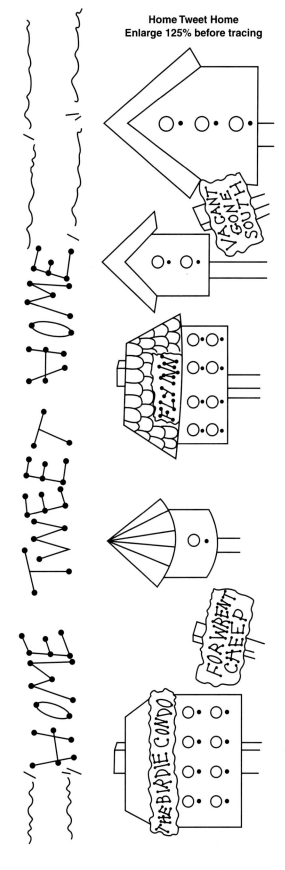

Home Tweet Home
Enlarge 125% before tracing

Southwestern Sizzle Note Cards

Designs by Mary Ayres

Materials

Set of Three Cards

- 4½" x 6" Earthtone cards with matching envelopes from Rubber Stampede: tan, off-white and medium green
- Scraps of solid papers: dark green, dark brown and off-white
- ZIG Memory System opaque gold writers from EK Success Ltd.: 6mm chisel tip and 0.5mm extra-fine tip
- Glue stick

Project Notes

Refer to photo and patterns throughout.

To transfer patterns, refer to instructions for "Using Transfer & Graphite Paper" in the General Instructions on page 190.

Instructions

1. Aligning dotted line along fold in card, transfer desired design onto front of note card, using tan card for cowboy boot, off-white for 10-gallon hat and medium green for cactus. Cut out shape along solid lines, leaving fold intact. (Do not cut out cactus tops.)

2. Cut accent pieces from solid papers, cutting boot top from dark green (cut out star), hatband from dark brown, and cactus tops from off-white.

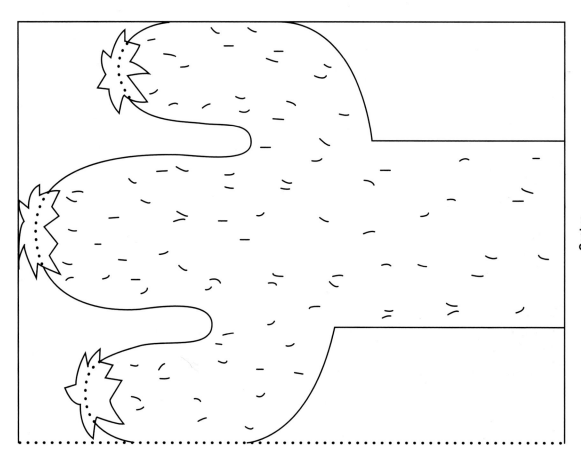

Cactus

3. Finish individual designs with gold markers and glue accent pieces in place with glue stick:

Cowboy boot: Draw along edges of boot and boot top with chisel-tip writer; glue boot top to boot. Add "stitching lines" with extra-fine-tip writer.

10-gallon hat: Draw along edges of hat and band with chisel-tip writer; glue hatband to hat. Add "stitching lines" with extra-fine-tip writer.

Cactus: Draw along edges of cactus with chisel-tip writer; completely color off-white cactus tops with chisel-tip writer and glue to top of cactus. Add cactus spines with extra-fine-tip writer.

4. Insert note cards in matching envelopes. ❀

For your next cookout or barbecue, round up a herd of your favorite friends with invitations issued on these simple but stylish notes in a trio of cowboy designs.

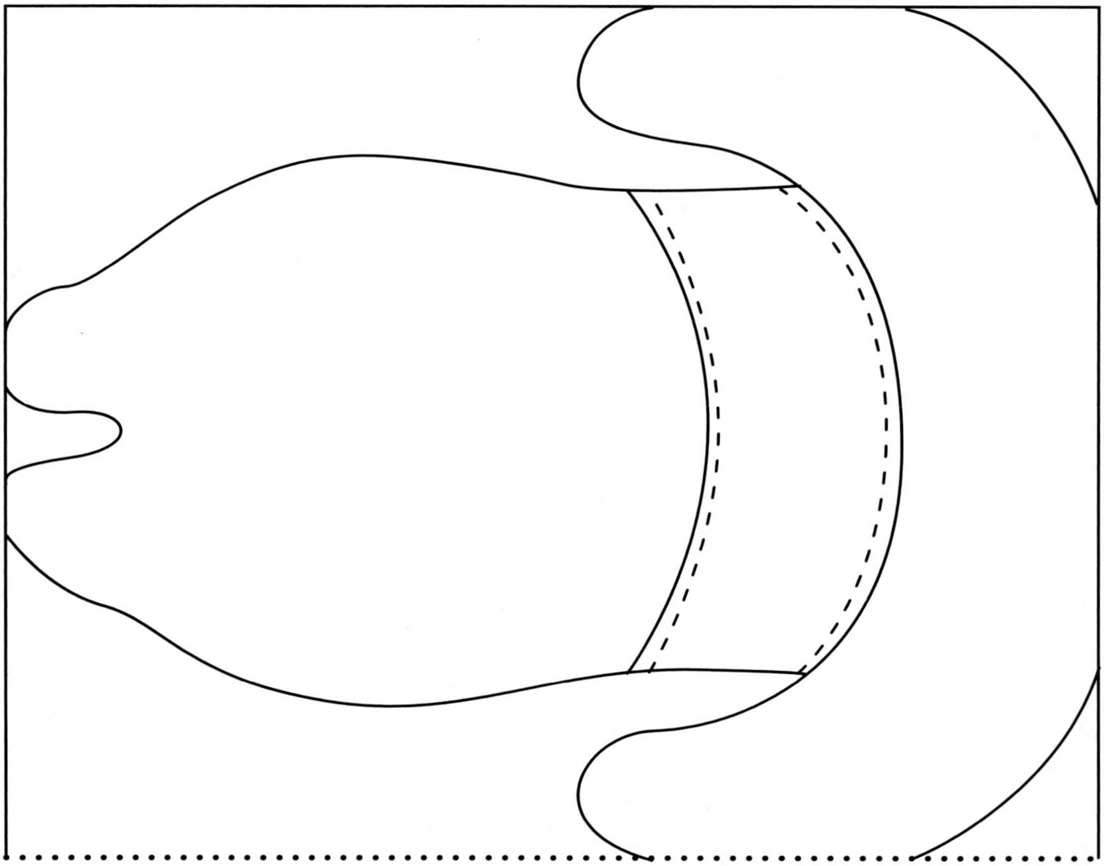

10-Gallon Hat

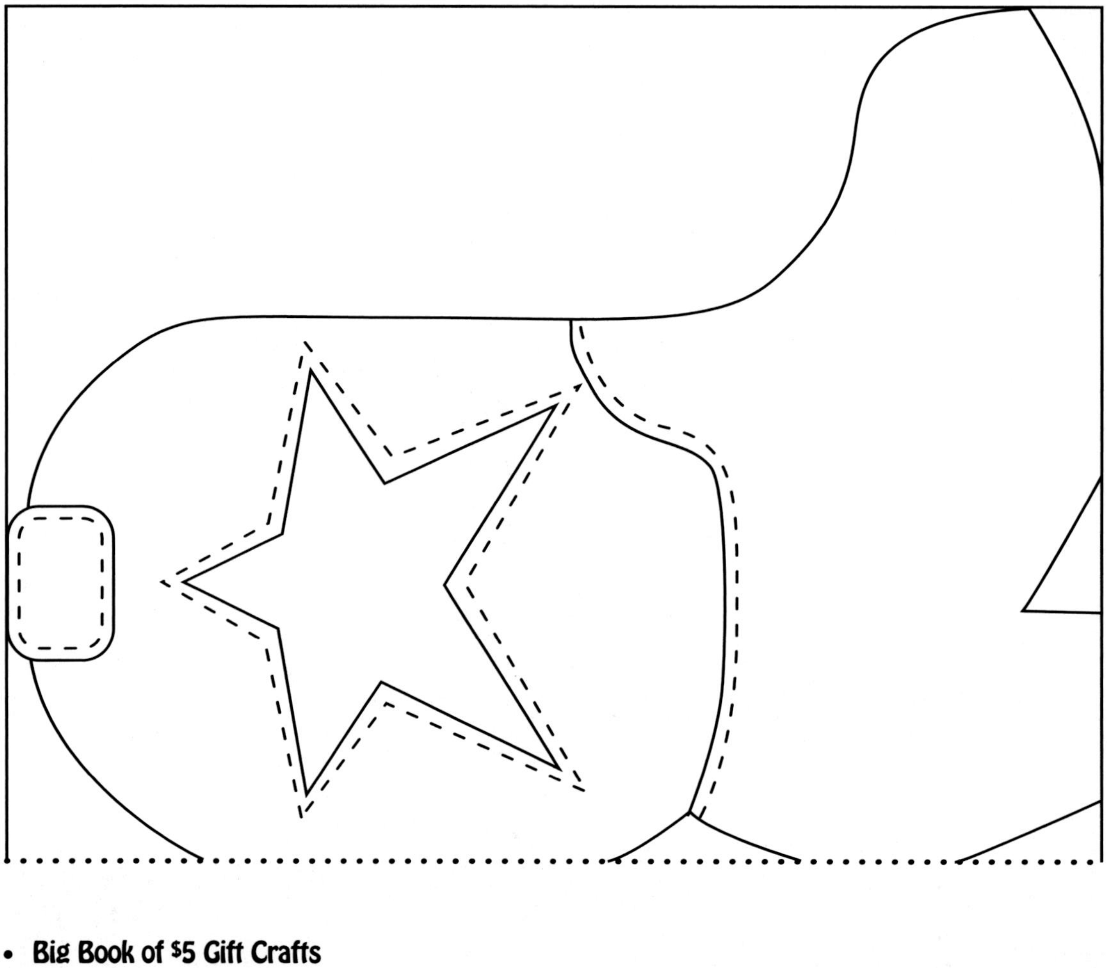

Cowboy Boot

These colorful bookmarks are so simple to make! Gift wrap and scrapbook papers are perfect for these designs.

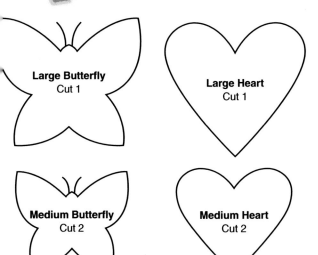

Large Butterfly
Cut 1

Medium Butterfly
Cut 2

Large Heart
Cut 1

Medium Heart
Cut 2

Hearts & Butterflies Bookmarks

Designs by Helen L. Rafson

Small Heart
Cut 2

Materials
Each Bookmark

- 2½" x 7" strip white art paper
- Wrapping paper
- Glue stick
- Pinking shears or decorative-edge scissors (optional)
- Clear contact paper
- ¼"-diameter round hole punch
- 5 (10") strands embroidery floss in coordinating color
- Black fine-point marker

Project Note
Refer to photo and patterns throughout.

Instructions
1. Cut one large heart, two medium hearts and two small hearts (or one large butterfly, two medium butterflies and one small butterfly) from wrapping paper.

2. Also from wrapping paper, cut two strips ⅜" x 7" and two strips ⅜" x 2½". Glue these strips to art paper to make border around bookmark. Trim edges of bookmark with pinking shears or decorative edge scissors, if desired.

3. Glue hearts or butterflies to front of bookmark. Using marker, draw antennae above butterfly shapes on butterfly bookmark.

4. Cut two pieces of contact paper 4½" x 9". Lay bookmark in center of one piece; cover with second piece of contact paper. Press with fingers to secure layers. Trim excess contact paper, leaving ⅛" border all around bookmark.

5. Punch hole at center top of bookmark. Hold embroidery floss strands together, ends even. Fold strands in half. Pull uncut end through hole; pass cut ends through loop and pull gently to secure knot. Trim tassel ends evenly. ❧

Small Butterfly
Cut 1

Happy House Warmers

There are many wonderful occasions for crafting an easy home decor project! Whether you wish to thank a hostess for a dinner invitation, or give a little something to a couple who has just bought their first home, this assortment of fun-to-craft items will be as delightful to craft as they are to share!

Bunny Welcome

Design by Mary Ayres

Materials

- 6¾" x 8¾" chalkboard with wooden frame
- Wooden pieces from Lara's Crafts: 4" x 7" angel and 5¾" x 2" banner/wing
- Wooden pieces from Forster: Woodsies 1" heart and 2 (1½") teardrops, and 2 jumbo craft sticks
- 4¼" x 5¼" wooden fence from Darice
- ¼" round wooden furniture plug
- 3" round Battenburg-and-fabric doily
- ⅜ yard ¼" blue satin ribbon
- Assorted small silk flowers
- Americana acrylic paints from DecoArt: white wash #DA2, lemon yellow #DA11, baby pink #DA31, baby blue #DA42, mink tan #DA92, milk chocolate #DA174, summer lilac #DA189, peony pink #DA215
- Paintbrushes: #6 and #8 round bristle, #6 soft round
- ZIG markers from EK Success Ltd.: black twin-tip permanent marker, opaque white extra-fine-tip writer, purple and wheat fine-tip permanent markers
- Tacky craft glue
- Fine sandpaper
- Transfer or graphite paper

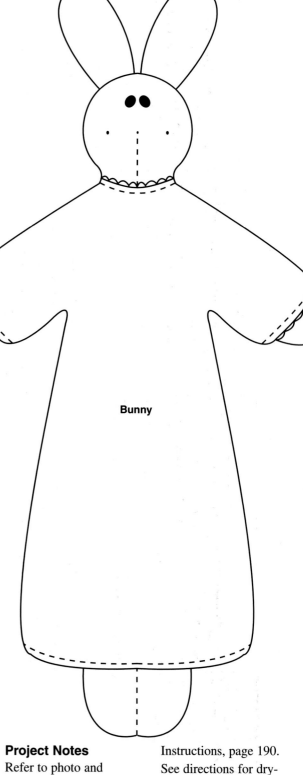

Bunny

Lettering

bunny and me

welcome

thee

Project Notes

Refer to photo and patterns throughout.

Let all paints and inks dry between applications.

For directions on transferring patterns, see "Using Transfer & Graphite Paper" in General Instructions, page 190.

See directions for drybrushing and rouging under "Painting Techniques" in General Instructions, page 191.

Instructions

1. Lightly sand wooden pieces as needed. Transfer

Paint this friendly bunny and her chalkboard cottage in bright colors to greet visitors. She's a delightful welcome gift for new neighbors.

edges of dress at cuffs and feet to bunny. Paint dress baby pink. Using tip of paintbrush handle, paint evenly spaced summer lilac dots on dress. Paint remainder of bunny and wooden teardrops (ears) mink tan.

2. Dry-brush edges of dress with mink tan and edges of bunny head, ears, hands and feet with milk chocolate. Paint wooden plug (nose) baby pink; dry-brush edges with peony pink.

3. Transfer face to bunny. Rouge cheeks and inner ears with peony pink. Using side of twin-tip marker's bullet tip, draw eyes; using fine tip, add stitching lines at dress cuffs, neckline and hem, and details on face and feet. Using opaque white writer throughout, add highlight dot to center of nose and cheeks; draw single line between dress and feet; add lacy details at cuffs and neckline.

4. *Apron:* Cut doily in half; glue one piece around bunny under arms with cut edge at top. Glue 3" piece of ribbon around bunny over top of apron; glue ends in back. Tie remaining ribbon in a bow; trim ends evenly and glue to center top of dress.

5. Glue nose to bunny; glue ears to back of bunny's head, points down.

6. Paint chalkboard frame

summer lilac. Draw wavy horizontal and vertical lines fairly close together using purple marker.

7. Paint banner insert baby blue; paint heart peony pink. Paint jumbo craft sticks (roof) lemon yellow; using wheat marker, draw wavy lines close together along length of craft sticks. Paint fence white wash. Dry-brush edges of all pieces painted in steps 6 and 7 with mink tan.

8. Transfer words

to upper right corner of chalkboard. Using opaque white writer, trace over words and add stitching line around chalkboard close to edges.

9. Glue assembled bunny to bottom left of chalkboard; glue fence to bottom right and over bunny. Glue flowers to bottom of fence. Glue baby blue

banner centered at top of chalkboard so that straight edge of banner overlaps about half of top of chalkboard frame. Glue jumbo craft sticks over top of house at an angle; glue heart in center of banner; let dry.

10. Using opaque white writer, draw stitching line on heart close to edge; draw straight stitching lines on baby blue roof insert radiating from heart. ❀

Floral Welcome Doorknob Hanger

Design by Kathy Wegner

Materials

- 3⅛" x 9½" wooden doorknob hanger
- Woodsies wooden cutouts from Forster: 10 medium circles, 4 small teardrops
- Aleene's all-purpose primer #EN 104
- Aleene's Premium-Coat acrylic paints: light pink #OC 101, light green #OC 137, light blue #OC 149, beige #OC 182
- Heavy-duty craft adhesive
- Fine-point permanent black marking pen
- Matte-finish spray varnish
- Sandpaper and tack cloth
- Foam paintbrush
- Paintbrush

Project Notes

Refer to photo throughout.

Let all coats of primer, ink, paints and varnish dry between applications.

Instructions

1. Sand wood; wipe with tack cloth. Using foam paintbrush, seal wood with primer; let dry. Sand lightly and wipe again with tack cloth.

2. Paint all surfaces of doorknob hanger with two coats beige paint.

3. Using paintbrush, paint one side and edges of wooden cutouts as follows: *light green*—four small teardrops; *light pink*—two medium circles; *medium blue*—eight medium circles. Set aside to dry.

4. Using black marking pen, add lettering and stitching lines.

5. Glue painted cutouts to door hanger with adhesive.

6. Spray sign with varnish. ✿

Greet new neighbors with a pretty door decoration quickly constructed from wooden cutouts and acrylic paints!

Dress up a mirror with blooming paper and a big bow for a pretty accent piece that will brighten any spot.

Project Note
Refer to photo throughout.

Instructions

1. Place floral paper right side up on top of foam-core board. Using pencil, mark foam-core to fit paper exactly. Cut off excess foam-core board.

2. Lightly coat front of foam-core board and back of floral paper with rubber cement; let dry to a dull finish. Carefully position floral paper on top of foam-core board so that it fits exactly.

3. Using craft knife, cut out center rectangle from floral paper, cutting all the way through foam-core board and paper.

4. Turn foam-core board over. Center oval mirror over opening. Trace around mirror with pencil. Set mirror aside and use craft knife to cut out mirror-shaped opening, being careful to cut only to the middle layer of the foam-core board. Remove all foam-core paper from the oval on the back. Using craft knife, carefully remove about ⅛" of foam-core from oval on back, trying to keep the surface as level as possible.

5. Paint outer edge of foam-core board and inner edge of mirror opening pale yellow; let dry.

6. Place mirror in oval opening on back of foam-core board; secure with masking tape.

7. Coat back of project and one side of white paper with rubber cement; let dry to dull finish. Place white paper on back of project so that they line up exactly.

8. Hot-glue paper twist around outer edge of project, starting at top center. For hanger, cut a 4" piece of paper twist from the end and fold it in half to form a loop; hot-glue to top center on back of project. Untwist about 28" piece; flatten and smooth with fingers. Tie in a bow; hot-glue bow to top center of project. Trim ends of streamers at an angle. ❀

Floral Mirror

Design by Tina Wheeler

Materials
- 1 sheet Amscan floral paper #41551
- 9" x 11½" piece white foam-core board
- Pale yellow #2005 Ceramcoat acrylic paint from Delta
- Paintbrush
- Craft knife with sharp pointed blade
- 4" x 6" oval mirror from Darice
- Hot-glue gun
- 80" lavender paper twist
- Masking tape
- 1 sheet plain white paper
- Wrinkle-free rubber cement

Strawberry Bucket

Design by Sandra Lee

Materials
- Galvanized tin bucket
- Krylon white primer
- Americana acrylic paints from DecoArt: titanium white #DA1, cadmium yellow #DA10, cadmium red #DA15, hi-lite flesh #DA24, burnt sienna #DA63, lamp black #DA67, true red #DA129, Hauser light green #DA131, Hauser dark green #DA133, Napa red #DA165
- Paintbrushes: #12 flat, 0 liner, #6 filbert
- Household vinegar
- Faux glazing medium
- Graphite or transfer paper
- Sealer

Project Notes
Smaller bucket shown is 4¼" high and 6" in diameter; larger bucket is 6⅛" high and 8½" in diameter.

Refer to instructions for transferring design under "Using Transfer & Graphite Paper" in General Instructions on page 190.

Refer to directions for base-coating, shading and highlighting under "Painting Techniques" in General Instructions on page 191.

Refer to photo and pattern throughout.

Instructions
1. Wash bucket in a solution of vinegar water; let dry. Spray with primer.

2. Transfer pattern onto bucket with graphite or transfer paper.

3. Paint different elements of design:

Leaves—Double-load flat brush with Hauser light green and Hauser dark green.

Strawberries—Base-coat strawberries with cadmium red. Double-load flat brush with glaze on one side and hi-lite flesh on the other side; highlight berries on one side near the fattest part. Shade one side of each berry with brush double-loaded with glaze on one side and true red on the other. Shade other side of each berry using a brush double-loaded with glaze on one side and Napa red on the other. Make shading on some berries deeper than on others. Don't be concerned about the shine left by the glaze; it will

disappear when final coat of sealer is applied.

Blossoms—Paint petals using filbert brush loaded with hi-lite flesh and lightly tipped in titanium white. Add blossom centers with cadmium yellow. When dry, shade bottoms of centers with brush double-loaded with glaze on one side and burnt sienna on the other.

Berry details—Combine small amounts of glaze, hi-lite flesh and water to make a mixture with an inky consistency. Using liner brush, add cross-hatching over berries without going all the way to the edge. (It will dry slightly lighter than it appears when wet.) Thin lamp black slightly with glaze and water; use mixture to add seeds to berries. Highlight one side of seeds with mixture of cadmium yellow, glaze and water. (The glaze keeps the paint full-bodied while still permitting the water to thin it slightly without running.)

Stems and leaf veins—Add using liner brush and Hauser dark green thinned to an inky consistency.

4. When completely dry, coat painted design with sealer. ❀

Strawberry Bucket

T in buckets dressed up with berries or flowers are pretty and practical catchalls!

Pink Dogwood Bucket Instructions begin on next page.

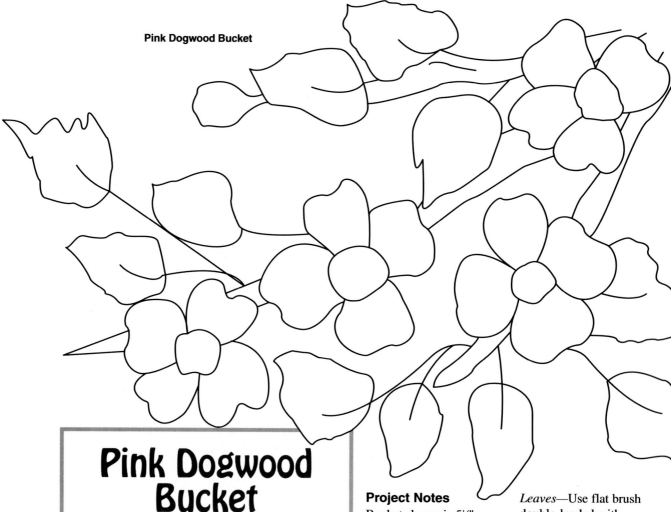

Pink Dogwood Bucket

Pink Dogwood Bucket

Design by Sandra Lee

Materials

- Galvanized tin bucket
- Krylon white primer
- Americana acrylic paints from DecoArt: titanium white #DA1, baby pink #DA31, dark chocolate #DA65, Hauser light green #DA131, Hauser dark green #DA133, black green #DA157, Napa red #DA165
- Paintbrushes: #1 script liner, #10 flat shader
- Toothpick
- Household vinegar
- Matte sealer

What a pretty gift this would make filled with seed packets or a plant!

Project Notes

Bucket shown is 5½" high and 6" in diameter.

Refer to directions for base-coating, shading and highlighting under "Painting Techniques" in General Instructions on page 191.

Refer to photo and pattern throughout.

Instructions

1. Wash bucket in a solution of vinegar water; let dry. Spray with primer.

2. Paint different elements of design:

Branches—Double-load flat brush with dark chocolate and titanium white.

Leaves—Use flat brush double-loaded with Hauser light green on one side and Hauser dark green on the other.

Dogwood blossoms— Leaving centers of blossoms open, paint four petals per flower with flat brush double-loaded with baby pink on one side and Napa red on the other. Fill in centers with black green. Using liner brush and Napa red, add V in end of each petal. Using toothpick dipped in Hauser light green, add a few dots over black green flower centers.

3. When completely dry, coat painted design with sealer. ✿

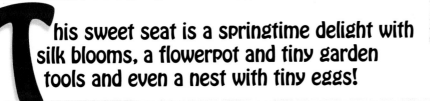

This sweet seat is a springtime delight with silk blooms, a flowerpot and tiny garden tools and even a nest with tiny eggs!

Woodland Twig Chair

Design by Creative Chi

Materials

- 3" x 3" x 11" twig "fairy chair"
- 12" piece cut from moss/gypso garland #NIC 7806 from Nicole Greenhouse Collection
- 1¾" straw hat
- Scrap of ⅛" pink ribbon
- Assorted small silk flowers
- 2" bird nest and coordinating eggs
- Assorted miniatures (see Project Notes)
- Hot-glue gun

Project Notes

Refer to photo throughout.

Miniatures used on sample include 1" flowerpot, 1½"trowel, gardening gloves, a snail, two birds and a miniature pot of flowers.

Instructions

1. Drape and glue garland around and through openings in chair as desired.

2. Line nest with a scrap of garland glued in place, then fill with eggs. Wrap ribbon around hat; tie bow and secure with flower. Glue bird's nest and hat to chair.

3. Glue assorted small flowers to garland; add miniatures as desired. ❀

Beach Treasures Gift Basket

Design by Creative Chi

Materials

- Seagrass basket with lid
- Scraps of dried Spanish moss and preserved greenery
- Small twigs
- Seashells: 1 large and 4 or 5 small
- 2 (6") lengths braided raffia
- 12" lengths paper twist ribbon: 1 each blue and green
- 6 (6mm) pearl beads
- Scraps of dried white statice or other small dried flowers
- Hot-glue gun

Decorate a graceful seagrass basket with seashells, tiny twigs reminiscent of driftwood, and faux pearls.

Project Note

Refer to photo throughout.

Instructions

1. Spread moss across top of basket and glue in place to form base for decorations.

2. Glue on greenery, then twigs and raffia braid. Form loops of paper twist ribbon; glue in place.

3. Glue large shell in center; glue smaller shells around edges of large one. Glue pearl beads and flowers around shells. ✿

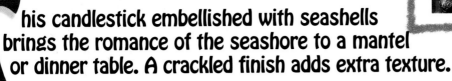

This candlestick embellished with seashells brings the romance of the seashore to a mantel or dinner table. A crackled finish adds extra texture.

Seashell Candlestick

Design by Barbara Woolley

Materials

- Unfinished 7" wooden candlestick
- Frosted glass votive holder to fit candlestick
- Assorted small seashells
- Craft cement
- 1 yard purple plastic-coated wire
- Aleene's Premium-Coat acrylic paints: deep peach #OC 116, deep sage #OC 134, deep spruce #OC 146, deep blue #OC 152, deep violet #OC 164, deep fuchsia #OC 170, ivory #OC 179
- Aleene's Enhancers: satin varnish #EN 102, mosaic crackle medium step 1 #EN 111, mosaic crackle medium step 2 #EN 112
- Paintbrushes: #8 round and #10 shader
- Fine sandpaper and tack cloth
- Drill with small bit
- Wire cutters
- Needle-nose pliers
- Votive candle
- Varnish

Instructions continued on page 46

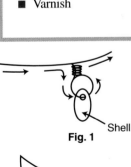

Shell

Fig. 1

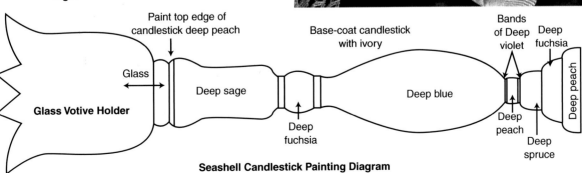

Paint top edge of candlestick deep peach

Base-coat candlestick with ivory

Bands of Deep violet

Deep fuchsia

Glass

Deep peach

Glass Votive Holder

Deep sage

Deep blue

Deep fuchsia

Deep peach

Deep spruce

Seashell Candlestick Painting Diagram

Pressed-Flower Suncatcher

Design by Fran Farris

Materials

- 2 (6") squares Aleene's crafting plastic
- Assorted pressed flowers from Nature's Pressed
- Silvered foil from Plaid
- Tweezers
- Sharp craft knife
- Toothpick
- White craft glue
- Hole punch
- Suction cup

Project Notes

Refer to photo throughout.

When arranging flowers, position any greenery and leaves first, and flowers last.

Instructions

1. Lay one square of plastic on a flat surface. Using tweezers, arrange pressed flowers and leaves as desired.

2. Using toothpick, apply tiny dots of craft glue to backs of flowers and leaves to secure them to plastic. Lay second square of plastic atop flower arrangement.

3. Cut even strips of silvered foil a bit longer than 6"; apply one to each edge of suncatcher. Trim edges, then repeat with a second layer of silvered foil edging along all edges.

4. Practice punching holes on scraps of plastic, then punch hole in top corner

Sandwich pressed flowers between craft plastic, then edge with silver foil strips!

of suncatcher. Hang suncatcher from suction cup in window. ✿

Seashell Candlestick continued from page 45

Project Notes

Refer to photo, painting diagram and Fig. 1 throughout.

Follow manufacturer's instructions for applying crackle medium.

Refer to directions for base-coating under "Painting Techniques" in General Instructions on page 191.

Instructions

1. Wash and dry glass votive holder. Cement small seashells around rim. Choose an especially nice one to cement to the center of the side of votive holder.

2. Sand candlestick lightly; remove dust with tack cloth. Base-coat candlestick with ivory; let dry.

3. Brush on one uneven coat of step 1 crackle medium; let dry.

4. Paint sections of candlestick as shown in photo and painting diagram. Allow time for paint to dry.

5. Apply a thick coat of mosaic crackle activator; let dry thoroughly at room temperature.

6. Apply one coat of varnish.

7. Drilling from inside to outside of shell, drill a small hole in each shell to be strung on wire. Attach shells to wire as shown in Fig. 1 using needle-nose pliers to crimp and twist wire.

8. Loop wire around bottom of candlestick; wrap wire with shells loosely around candlestick to top. Form loop in opposite end of wire to fit around bottom of votive; insert votive candle in candle holder with wire loop attached. ✿

 ecorate a recycled jar with paints and fabric scraps, then fill with candies or other treats for a delightful gift.

Project Notes

Refer to photo and pattern throughout.

Let all paints dry between applications.

Follow manufacturer's instructions for using transfer web.

Instructions

1. Trace pattern onto tracing paper. Cut out to fit on top of lid. Tape pattern in place.

2. Place lid on protective surface. Use hammer to tap nail from dot to dot, piercing lid. Change nail when point dulls.

3. Hold up punched lid to light; repunch any holes where necessary. Remove pattern and tape.

4. Paint designs inside punched lines using thick strokes: *white*—center of apple; *red*—outer portion of apple; *green*—leaf; *brown*—stem.

5. Using fine-point black marker, add three apple seeds to center of apple.

6. Fuse transfer web onto back of fabric. Cut out several apples; peel off paper backing and fuse to sides of glass jar with hot iron. ❀

Apple for the Teacher

Apple for the Teacher

Design by Sandra Graham Smith

Materials

- 10-ounce glass jar with plain metal lid
- ¼ yard Dream Spinners apple print fabric from V.I.P.
- ¼ yard heavy-duty Wonder Under transfer web from Pellon
- Glossy enamel paints: white, red, green and brown
- Small artist paintbrush
- Pressed-wood board or other hard, protective surface
- Hammer
- Several finishing nails
- Tracing paper
- Masking tape
- Black fine-point permanent marking pen
- Iron

Golden Glitter Gel Candle

Design by Vicki Blizzard

Materials

- 4 ounces clear Gel Candle by Delta
- 6" wick by Delta
- Scent by Delta (optional)
- Iridescent and gold candle glitter by Delta
- Recycled glass jar approximately 3" tall by 3" in diameter
- 36" 24-gauge gold craft wire
- 30–40 red glass cabochons (used for floral arrangements)
- Pencil or wooden skewer
- Heavy saucepan

Project Note

Refer to photo throughout.

Instructions

1. Following manufacturer's instructions, melt gel in heavy saucepan. Cool gel slightly and add approximately ½ teaspoon each of iridescent and gold glitter. If desired, stir in a few drops of scent.

2. Dip metal bottom of wick into gel and press into center of bottom of jar.

3. Wrap wire into a loose coil approximately 2½" in diameter. Set aside.

4. Holding wick out of the way, pour a thin layer of gel into bottom of jar and swirl it approximately 1" up sides of jar.

5. Working quickly to prevent gel from cooling, place wire coil in jar and place red glass cabochons on top of coil, holding it in place.

6. Wrap top of wick around pencil or wooden skewer to hold it in the center of jar. Fill jar with glittering gel to approximately ½" from top. Let gel cool completely. Trim wick to ¼" before burning candle. ✿

Golden wire and iridescent glitter add to the enchantment of this gel candle!

G ive a summer party a festive glow with this pair of colorful gel candles!

Summer Sherbet Candles

Designs by Laura Scott

Materials

- Gel Candle by Delta: 2 ounces each crystal, sapphire and peridot, and 4 ounces aquamarine
- 2 (10") wicks by Delta
- Candle scent by Delta (optional)
- Two tall, clear glass glasses, approximately 6" tall with 2½"-diameter openings
- 4 ceramic plates
- Sharp knife or scissors
- 4 heavy saucepans

Project Note

Refer to photo throughout.

Instructions

1. Following manufacturer's instructions, melt each color of gel in a separate heavy saucepan. If desired, after removing gel from stove, add scent to melted gel.

2. Pour each color of gel onto a separate ceramic plate in a ¼"-thick layer to cool.

3. When cool, cut each color into small pieces by slicing into ¼"-wide strips, then dicing vertically.

4. Dip the metal tab from one wick in melted crystal gel; stick it in the center bottom of one glass. Repeat with remaining wick and glass.

5. Using spoon or fingers, fill glass with gel pieces as shown or as desired. ❀

Kitty-Cat Pot Holders

Design by Mary Ayres

Materials

- 100-percent cotton fabrics: scraps of 4 different homespuns or plaids for border, scrap for cat, 5½" square of off-white solid, and 7½" square of one of the border fabrics
- ¾"-wide flat heart-shaped button
- Warm & Natural needled cotton batting
- HeatnBond Ultra Hold iron-on adhesive from Therm O Web
- 1¼ yards black jumbo rickrack
- 6-strand embroidery floss: black, white and color to match cat fabric
- Sewing threads: black and blue
- Embroidery and hand-sewing needles
- Mat, Lucite ruler and rotary cutter

Project Notes

Refer to photo and pattern throughout.

Follow manufacturer's instructions for fusing iron-on adhesive.

Stitch seams using ¼" seam allowance. Press seams to one side, generally to the side with less bulk.

Instructions

1. Cut iron-on adhesive slightly larger than pattern for kitty cat. Fuse to back of cat fabric; cut out kitty cat and peel off paper backing.

2. Position kitty on off-white center block. Design should be centered from side to side and bottom edge of head should be even with bottom edge of off-white block. Fuse kitty cat to off-white fabric.

3. *Log cabin border:* From each homespun fabric, cut one of the following strips: 1½" x 5½", two 1½" x 6½", and one 1½" x 7½". Sew 5½" strip to top of center block. Sew one 6½" strip to right side and the other to the bottom of center block. Sew 7½" strip to left side of center block.

4. *Embroidery:* Work blanket stitch around top and side edges of kitty cat using 3 strands matching floss. Using 2 strands black floss, embroider mouth and vertical line on muzzle with stem stitch. For dots on muzzle, work French knots using 1 strand black floss wrapped around needle three times. For eyes, work French knots using 3 strands black floss wrapped around needle four times. Using white embroidery floss, sew heart button at top of vertical muzzle line for nose.

5. Cut two 7½" squares from cotton batting. Baste squares to wrong side of pot holder front. Stitching through center of rickrack, sew rickrack around front edges of pot holder, beginning and ending in top left corner.

6. *Hanging loop:* Cut 4¼" piece black jumbo rickrack; fold in half and baste ends to top left corner of pot holder.

7. Lay pot holder front atop 7½" fabric square for backing, right sides facing, and stitch together along rickrack stitching, leaving 4" opening at bottom for turning. Trim corners; turn pot holder right side out and hand-stitch opening closed. ✿

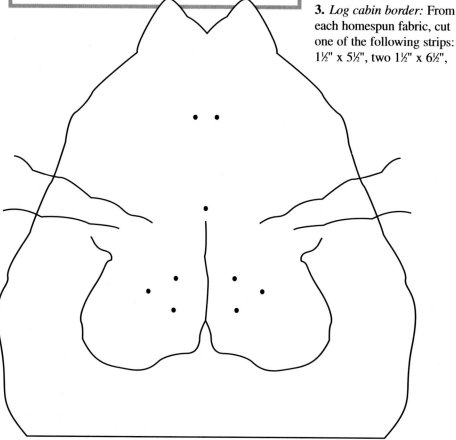

B

right, unmatched prints and plaids in the border strips give this precious puss a fresh, whimsical look. You'll have a ball making these!

D ress up a room with stylish accessories featuring grapes-and-leaves motifs.

Bountiful Grapes Accessories

Designs by Kim Lasky

Materials
- Products from Pop-Up Paper: lamp shade cover, wastepaper basket, small picture frame, tissue box cover, single and double switchplate covers
- Decorator glaze paints from Plaid: white, russet brown, plum, deep purple, ivy green, deep woods green, new gold leaf
- Grapevine #53203 decorator block from Plaid
- Paintbrushes: ¾" flat, #1 script liner
- Small sea sponge

Project Notes
Refer to photo throughout.

Use ¾" flat brush unless instructed otherwise.

For block printing (steps 4 and 5), refer to directions accompanying decorator block kit.

Instructions
1. Paint all surfaces russet brown, randomly applying paint heavily to some areas and lightly to others.

2. Using small sea sponge that has been moistened, lightly sponge the entire surface with white. Let dry.

3. Randomly brush surface lightly with new gold leaf.

4. Block-print grapes using plum and deep purple.

5. Block-print leaves using ivy green and deep woods green; add tendrils and veins using #1 script liner. ❀

Glass Jar Banks

Design by Ann Butler

Add a few coins to one of these quick-and-easy banks for a thoughtful and useful gift.

Materials

- Clean jar with lid
- Krylon interior/exterior spray paint
- Your choice of fabric
- Raffia or ribbon
- White acrylic paint
- Old toothbrush
- Double-edge chisel or large flathead screwdriver
- Hammer
- Black permanent marking pen (optional)
- Small piece of wood to fit inside jar lid
- Craft glue
- Pinking shears

Project Note

Refer to photo throughout.

Instructions

1. Place lid on jar; spray entire lid and jar, including bottom, with two coats of paint, letting paint dry between coats.

2. Remove lid; position lid right side up on small piece of wood. Using chisel and hammer, punch a 1½" opening in center of lid. Remove wood; pound cut edges of lid flat against inside of lid.

3. Using pinking shears, cut fabric motif(s) as desired; glue onto jar.

4. Spatter-paint jar, including lid and bottom, with white paint and toothbrush; let dry.

5. Tie raffia or ribbon bow around jar.

6. *Optional:* Write words—"Pin Money," "Slush Fund," etc.—on fabric with marking pen. ❁

et's face it: A flyswatter is a necessity in many homes—and it's not a pretty sight! But here's a clever way to camouflage it with color!

Easy Foam Swatter Bonnets

Designs by Mary Ayres

Materials

Both Bonnets

- 2 flyswatters
- Craft foam from Fibre-Craft: blue, yellow, orange, rainbow colors and shades-of-blue
- Medium-tip black permanent marker
- ⅛" round hole punch from Fiskars
- Black craft cord
- Pinking and wave-edge paper edgers
- Transparent circle and starburst templates from C-Thru Ruler Co.
- Tacky craft glue

Butterfly Swatter Bonnet

Instructions continued on page 57

Felt Nosegay Pocket

Design by Angie Wilhite

Materials

- ⅞" Woodsies wooden star cutout from Forster
- Blue acrylic paint
- Paintbrush
- Rainbow Felt Classic from Kunin Felt: 4" x 8" antique white, 5" square cranberry, 5" square denim
- Embroidery floss in cream and blue to match felt
- 8" piece ⅛"-wide burgundy satin ribbon to match cranberry felt
- Pellon products: 8" square Wonder-Under transfer web, 6" square Fusible Fleece, 2" square Craft-Bond adhesive
- Fabric glue
- Small bunch of silk burgundy flowers
- Iron and pressing cloth

Here's a perfect "little something" to dress up a bare spot in your country home!

Project Notes

Refer to photo and pattern throughout.

Follow manufacturer's instructions for using transfer web, fusible fleece and adhesive.

Use 2 strands floss for all embroidery.

Instructions

1. Paint star cutout blue; set aside to dry.

2. Apply adhesive to wrong side of a 2" square of cranberry felt; cut birdhouse opening from felt.

3. Apply fusible fleece to wrong side of denim felt; apply transfer web to fleeced side of denim felt and to wrong side of remaining cranberry felt. Cut birdhouse from denim felt and roof from cranberry.

4. Remove paper backing from birdhouse; position on right side of one antique white pocket; cover with pressing cloth and fuse in place.

5. Using cream floss through step 6, sew birdhouse opening to birdhouse with a single straight stitch in the center. Blanket-stitch around curved sides of birdhouse.

6. Remove paper backing from roof; cover with pressing cloth and fuse in place. Blanket-stitch around roof.

7. Using 2 strands blue floss throughout, blanket-stitch across top edge of pocket with birdhouse; holding pockets together, wrong sides facing, blanket-stitch together around curved edges. ✿

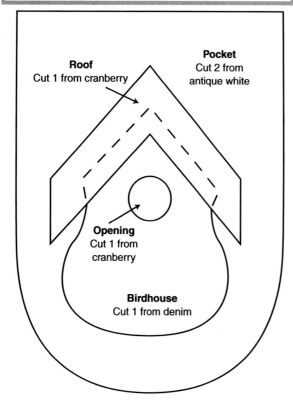

Pocket
Cut 2 from antique white

Roof
Cut 1 from cranberry

Opening
Cut 1 from cranberry

Birdhouse
Cut 1 from denim

Felt Nosegay Pocket

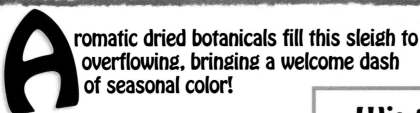

A romatic dried botanicals fill this sleigh to overflowing, bringing a welcome dash of seasonal color!

Project Note
Refer to photo throughout.

Instructions
1. Break off branches of princess pine; glue into sleigh to begin filling it out.

2. Glue cinnamon sticks into sleigh, breaking several into pieces of different lengths.

3. Add sprigs of green and white milo berries, then red eucalyptus bells.

4. Glue in hemlock cones, casuarina pods and star anise.

5. Tie ribbon in a bow; glue to outside of sleigh so streamers appear to ripple down side of sleigh. ❀

Winter Sleigh
Design by Creative Chi

Materials
- 5½" x 4½" x 2½" wicker sleigh
- Small bunch of dried princess pine
- 8 (3") cinnamon sticks
- 6 sprigs green milo berries
- 10 sprigs white milo berries
- 8 sprigs red eucalyptus bells
- 4 hemlock cones
- 3 casuarina pods
- 6 star anise
  - 18" piece ½"-wide red grosgrain ribbon
  - Hot-glue gun

Easy Foam Swatter Bonnets continued from page 55

Project Note
Refer to photo and pattern throughout.

Butterfly
1. Using pinking paper edgers, cut swatter bonnet from blue craft foam. Using wave-edge paper edgers along outside of wings and scissors along inside (body), cut butterfly wings from rainbow foam.

2. Using marker, draw evenly spaced dots around edges of all three pieces and add antennae to bonnet.

3. Glue wings to bonnet. Let dry.

4. Using hole punch, punch a hole in top square corners of bonnet. Place bonnet on top of fly swatter and bend squared corners over to back. Run cord through punched holes and through mesh of fly swatter and knot to secure. Weight flyswatter overnight with a heavy book or similar object to flatten craft foam.

Sunburst
1. Referring to pattern for butterfly swatter bonnet and using wave-edge paper edgers, cut swatter bonnet from shades-of-blue craft foam. Using regular scissors and templates, cut 3" circle from yellow foam and 4" starburst from orange.

2. Using marker, draw evenly spaced dots around edges of all three pieces.

3. Glue starburst to center bottom of bonnet, ⅞" above edge. Glue circle to center of starburst. Let dry.

4. Repeat step 4 as for butterfly bonnet. ❀

Watering Can With Mini-Utensils

Design by Deborah Spofford

Materials

- Wooden products from IKEA: mini utensil set #DUKTIG and watering can #NLD 199946
- Ceramcoat acrylic paints from Delta: blue heaven #2037, apple green #2065, pineapple yellow #2101, hydrangea pink #2449, white #2505
- Air-Dry PermEnamel paints from Delta: light blue and citrus yellow
- Acrylic gloss varnish from Delta
- Paintbrushes: #6 and #10 shaders, ⅝" glaze, #1 and #5 rounds
- Pencil
- Tracing paper
- Transfer paper
- Black permanent marker

Project Notes

Refer to photo and patterns throughout.

When transferring designs to utensils (step 2), refer to "Using Transfer & Graphite Paper" in General Instructions on page 190.

Instructions

1. Using #10 shader, paint spoon with a mixture of two parts apple green and one part white. Paint spatula blue heaven; paint perforated spoon hydrangea pink; paint scoop pineapple yellow. Let dry.

2. Transfer designs onto utensils using transfer paper.

3. Using #5 round and hydrangea pink throughout, paint dots on spatula and small flower on scoop.

4. Using #6 shader throughout and hydrangea pink, paint lines on scoop. Using apple green, paint stripes around handle of perforated spoon and flower around hole on one side of spoon.

5. Using #1 round brush and blue heaven throughout, paint blue dots randomly on handle of spoon and swirl in bowl of spoon; make small dots on handle of perforated spoon and lines around flower. Paint a solid blue flower around hole on other side of spoon. Paint a small dot in center of flower on scoop. Let all paints dry.

6. Using ⅝" glaze brush, coat utensils with varnish; let dry.

7. Trace flower onto front and back of watering can. Paint flower with light blue using #5 round brush; paint light blue stripes on spout and wavy line on handle with #6 shader. Let dry.

8. Using citrus yellow, paint center on flower; let dry.

9. Add details to flower with black permanent marker. ❀

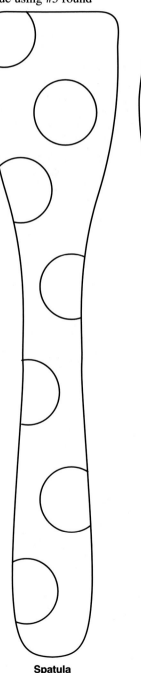

Spatula

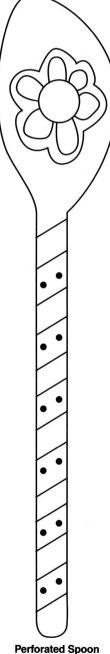

Perforated Spoon

Kids will love playing with these toy utensils and watering can, brightly painted with flowers, dots and swirls.

Scoop

Watering Can Flower

Spoon

Glittering Wings Note Cards

Designs by Barbara Woolley

Materials

Five Note Cards with Envelopes and Gift Bag

- Paper products from Bemiss-Jason Corp.: 5 (12" x 18") sheets natural Waffle paper, and 2 (12" x 16") sheets natural Wavy Ridges paper
- 12" x 28" piece 60-pound natural kraft postal wrap
- 1 sheet black rice paper
- 9½" x 12" light copper sheet from ArtEmboss
- Wooden and ball point styluses
- 6" square tracing paper
- Heavy-duty craft adhesive
- 20" piece jute twine
- Black acrylic paint
- White tacky glue
- ¼" round hole punch
- Masking tape
- Sharp scissors
- Paper towels
- Ruler

Small Butterfly

Project Notes

Refer to photo and patterns throughout.

Use white tacky glue for gluing all paper; use craft adhesive to cement copper butterflies to bag and note cards.

If black rice paper is hard to tear, moisten area to be torn.

Paper cut from a smooth, heavy, unprinted grocery bag can be substituted for kraft paper.

Embossing Butterfly

1. Photocopy large butterfly pattern or trace onto tracing paper. Place copper sheet right side up on old magazine. Lay butterfly pattern on copper and tape in place. Trace over pattern lines with fine end of ball point stylus. Remove pattern.

2. Turn copper over and, still using magazine as work surface, retrace around the pattern lines several times, using the larger end of the ball point stylus and the wooden stylus to "push" the copper into a "puffy" dimensional shape.

3. Turn copper back over so right side is up; cut out butterfly with sharp scissors leaving a ⅛" margin around butterfly.

4. Apply black paint to right side of butterfly with paper towel; wait for about 5 minutes, then wipe off paint with paper towel, leaving paint in embossed ridges. Set butterfly aside.

Gift Bag

1. Cut 16" x 8" rectangle from waffle paper. Turn paper wrong side up.

2. Referring to Fig. 1, use ruler to sketch fold lines (dashed lines) and cut lines (bold lines).

3. Using small end of ball point stylus and ruler, score all fold lines on wrong side of paper. This will permit sharp, crisp folds. Cut the four 1½" slits along bottom edge.

4. Fold down top 1" cuff to inside of bag; secure with glue. Fold paper into bag shape, gluing Flap A under Flap B. Fold up bottom flaps; glue in place.

5. Punch four holes in top cuff to receive jute handles. Cut jute in half; insert ends of one piece through punched holes on one side of bag from outside to inside; knot each end inside bag. Repeat on other side with remaining jute.

6. Cut 4" square from wavy ridges paper; glue to one side of gift bag. Tear a piece from black rice paper; glue to wavy ridges paper. Cement copper butterfly to rice paper.

Note Cards

1. Cut a 7½" x 4¾" rectangle from 60-pound kraft postal wrap. Using ruler and small end of ball point stylus, score a fold line on wrong side of paper so you can fold card in half into a 3¾" x 4¾" note card.

2. Cut a 3½" x 3" rectangle from wavy ridges paper; glue to front of note card. Top with a piece torn from black rice paper.

3. Referring to steps 1–4 for Embossing Butterfly and using pattern for small butterfly, make a butterfly and cement it to black rice paper. Repeat for remaining note cards.

Envelopes

1. Cut envelope pattern

Large Butterfly

Embossed copper adds sparkle to these distinctive notes. Present the set in a "shopping bag" of textured paper.

from waffle paper; turn paper wrong side up. Score along fold lines (dashed lines) using small end of ball point stylus and ruler.

2. Fold Flaps A to inside; apply glue to exposed surfaces of Flap A and fold up Flap B; press to secure. Fold down Flap C to complete envelope; tuck envelopes and note cards into gift bag. ❀

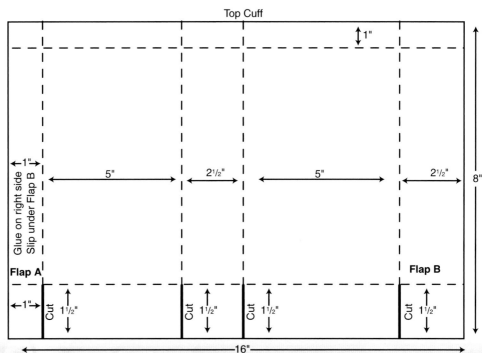

Top Cuff

1"

Glue on right side
Slip under Flap B

1"

5"

2½"

5"

2½"

8"

Flap A

Flap B

1"

Cut

1½"

Cut

1½"

Cut

1½"

Cut

1½"

16"

Fold along dashed lines

Bottom

**Fig. 1
Gift Bag**

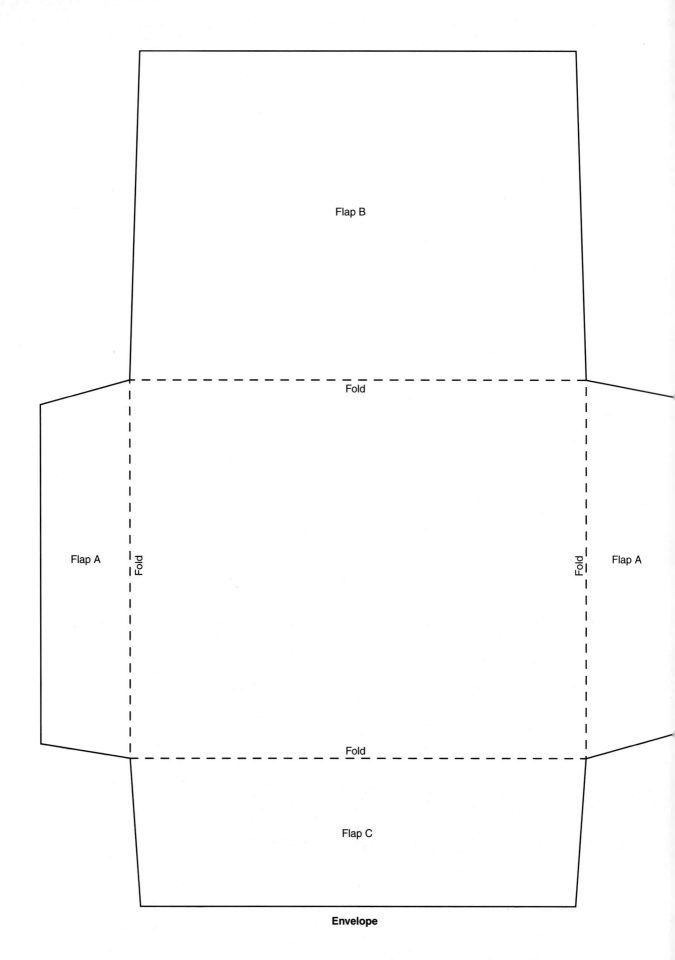

Flap B

Fold

Flap A

Fold

Fold

Flap A

Fold

Flap C

Envelope

Dress up that welcoming dish for your new neighbors with these fun and funky kitchen accessories!

Project Notes

Refer to photo throughout.

Using paint on rubber stamps: For best results, apply paint to stamp with a stencil sponge. Dip sponge in paint and then pat paint onto stamp. This helps control the amount of paint on the stamp.

Instructions

1. Wrap painters' tape around spoon handle 7" from end, and around paddle about 5" from end.

2. Paint handles periwinkle blue; remove tape before paint dries and let paint dry completely.

3. Apply apple green paint to swirl on the coffee stamp (see Project Notes). (If desired, cut swirl off stamp to make it easier to use.) Stamp swirls randomly over painted surface of paddle handle; let dry. Repeat with leaf stamp on spoon handle.

4. Coat painted handles with varnish; let dry.

5. Center one piece of wire on handle of spoon where paint ends; wrap around handle three times. Curl wire ends—about 7" each—around pencil or paintbrush handle, adding six or seven beads as you curl the wire. Using needle-nose pliers, curl ends so no sharp tips protrude. Repeat with remaining wire and beads on paddle handle. ❦

Beaded Kitchen Utensils

Design by Deborah Spofford

Materials

- Wooden utensil set #REDSKAP from IKEA
- 2 (18") pieces blue 20-gauge wire
- Ceramcoat acrylic paints from Delta: apple green #2065, periwinkle blue #2478
- Acrylic gloss varnish from Delta
- Paintbrushes: #6 shader, ⅜" glaze
- Approximately 13 assorted blue and green glass beads
- Rubber stamps from Rubber Stampede: coffee cup with swirl #72059, accent leaf #71006
- Stencil sponge
- Needle-nose pliers or wire cutters
- 1"-wide painters' tape

Celebrate Love

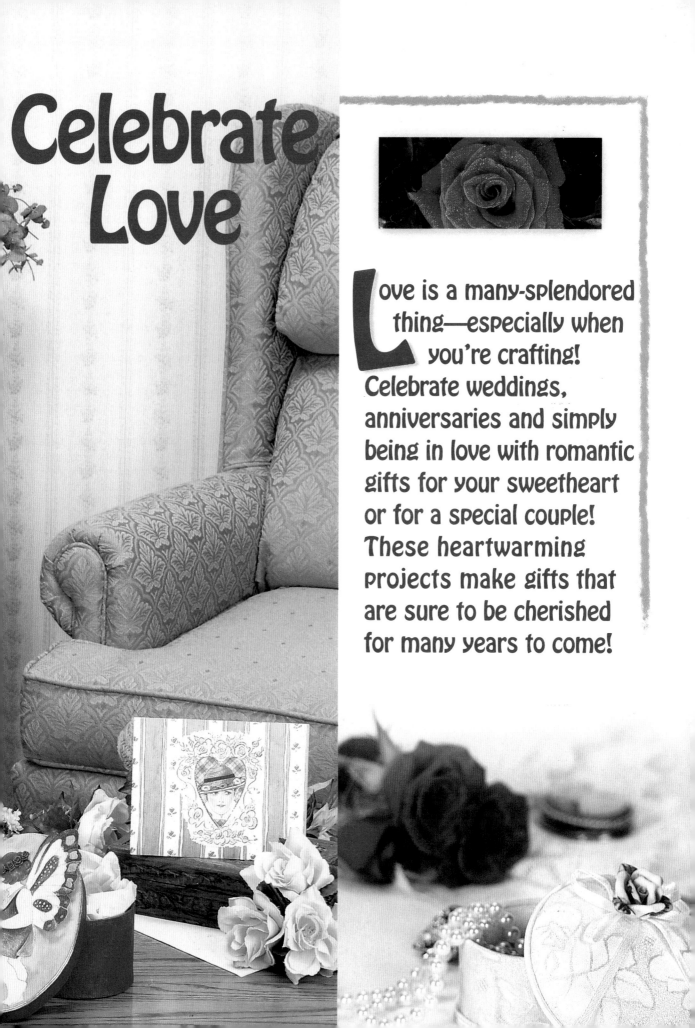

Love is a many-splendored thing—especially when you're crafting! Celebrate weddings, anniversaries and simply being in love with romantic gifts for your sweetheart or for a special couple! These heartwarming projects make gifts that are sure to be cherished for many years to come!

Winged Fairy Trinket Box

Design by June Fiechter

Materials

- 7½" x 5¾" x 3" oval papier-mâché box with lid #28-4183-000 from D&CC
- 8" square Kreative Kanvas from Kunin Felt
- Ceramcoat acrylic paints from Delta*: flesh-tone #2019, spice brown #2049, tompte red #2107, Cape Cod blue #2133
- Metallic 14K gold #2604 Ceramcoat Gleams paint from Delta*
- Ceramcoat Pearl Luster medium #224 from Delta
- Gold Hi Lustre #002HL very fine (#4) metallic braid from Kreinik
- 21" flat metallic gold braid
- Paintbrushes
- Small needle
- 5 (⅜") mauve ribbon rosettes
- Graphite transfer paper from Walnut Hollow
- Tacky craft glue
- Hot-glue gun

These colors are also available from Delta in a single collection as a Ceramcoat Super Pack.

Project Notes

Refer to photo throughout.

Refer to directions for transferring pattern under "Using Transfer & Graphite Paper" in the General Instructions on page 190.

Let all paints dry between applications.

Painting Fairy

1. Using transfer paper, transfer outline oval and entire picture *except wings* onto canvas. Cut out along oval outline. Very carefully, cut a slit along back edge only of collar and arm; wings will be inserted here later.

2. Transfer wings onto canvas, adding a ½" tab where they will be inserted; cut out.

3. Paint outer edges and center sections of wings with a mixture of equal parts tompte red and pearl luster. Dot painted center sections with a mixture of equal parts pearl luster and 14K gold (these dots are not shown on pattern). Paint "blocks" and dots in painted outer edges with undiluted 14K gold. Paint center sections of wings with pearl luster.

4. Paint background oval with a mixture of equal parts of pearl luster and Cape Cod blue.

5. Paint bow and fairy's dress (not collar) with *Continued on page 83*

Brandishing a scarlet bow and golden arrow à la Cupid, this sweet fairy brings a message of love to anyone lucky enough to receive her.

Winged Fairy Trinket Box

Guardian Angel Pin

Design by Paula Bales

Materials

- Forster Woodsies wooden pieces: medium circle, 2 small circles, large egg, 2 large wings
- Apple Barrel acrylic paints from Plaid: berry red, white, creamy peach, regency blue, black
- Paintbrushes: #4 shader, 5/0 spotter
- Cotton-tip swab or stencil brush
- Toothpick
- 10" Toner Plastics licorice 24-gauge Fun Wire
- ZIG .05 black Millennium marker from EK Success Ltd.
- 1" pin back
- Tacky glue or hot-glue gun
- Wire cutters

Project Notes

Refer to photo throughout.

Paint all surfaces of wooden pieces.

Let paints and ink dry between applications.

Instructions

1. *Head:* Paint medium circle creamy peach. Using tip of paintbrush handle, dot on two black eyes; dot on a slightly smaller berry red nose. Use tip of toothpick to dot a tiny white highlight dot onto each eye. Using swab or stencil brush, lightly apply cheeks with berry red. Using marker, outline head; draw mouth, eyebrows and eye details.

2. *Hair:* Cut wire into 10 1" pieces; curl one end of each. Glue straight ends to back of head for hair.

3. *Hands:* Paint small circles creamy peach. Outline with black marker.

4. *Wings:* Paint wings white; add thin stripes of regency blue to each. Outline wings with marker.

5. *Body:* Paint large egg regency blue. Using toothpick dipped in paint, dot on clusters of three white dots; add single dots of berry red between clusters. Outline body with marker.

6. Glue head and hands to right side of body, gluing head over pointed end. Glue wings to wrong side of body. Glue pin back to back of angel. ❀

T his sweet little token of affection is a touching reminder that you keep the wearer in your mind and heart.

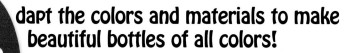

Adapt the colors and materials to make beautiful bottles of all colors!

Beaded Glass Bottle

Design by Judy Atwell

Materials

- 8" pale aqua bottle with cork stopper
- 25–30 (12mm) glass disc beads with matte finish
- Spool of aqua thread
- 1 strand dark blue-green glass seed beads
- Flat glass opalescent "marble"
- Size 0 nylon beading thread
- Tacky craft glue
- Twisted wire beading needle
- 8" x 5" piece cardboard

Project Note

Refer to photo throughout.

Instructions

1. Wash bottle with soap and water; rinse well. Dry upside down in rack.

2. Lay bottle flat. Using small amounts of glue, glue half of disc beads to one side of bottle, applying them like random polka dots rather than in lines. Let dry.

3. Repeat step 2 on opposite side of bottle.

4. Wind thread around 8" side of cardboard 100 times; cut one end; you should have 100 (16") pieces of thread. Hold them together in a hank and tie them around the neck of the bottle. Knot thread so thread ends are uneven. Secure knot with a dot of glue.

5. Glue flat side of marble to top of cork stopper.

6. Thread beading needle with two 36" pieces aqua thread. Double threads in needle and knot four ends together. Tie knot large enough to keep seed beads from sliding off. String about 1" of seed beads, then one disc bead, then 5" of seed beads. Push needle through knot of thread on neck of bottle; thread on about 4" of seed beads, a disc bead and 1" of seed beads. End with a large knot. ❀

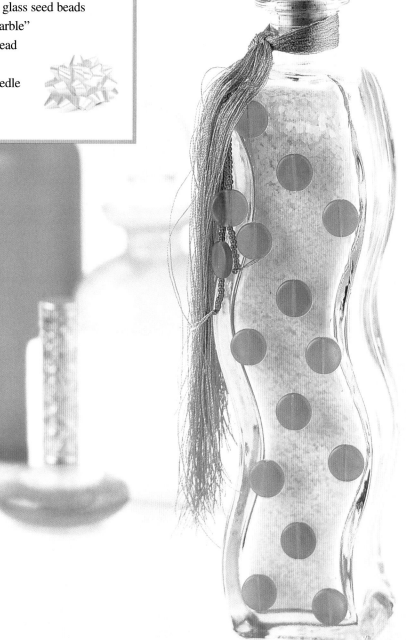

Lovely Lacy Hangers

Design by Charlyne Stewart

Materials

Each Hanger

- Wooden hanger with metal hook
- ⅛ ounce powder blue synthetic four-ply yarn
- 1 yard 5"-wide white scallop-edge lace trim
- ¼ yard powder blue felt
- White sewing and quilting threads
- Sewing machine with open toe and walking feet
- 1 yard 1½"-wide white satin ribbon with metallic gold edging
- 6" ³⁄₁₆"-wide white satin ribbon
- White craft glue
- Seam sealant

Project Note

Refer to photo and pattern throughout.

Hanger

1. Apply white glue to hanger hook. Wrap tightly and evenly with yarn, knotting it at the end of hook and concealing yarn ends under wrapping. Let dry thoroughly.

2. Cut two hanger covers on the fold from powder blue felt and from scall op-edge lace. Instead of cutting the bottom edge as a straight line (as shown on pattern), cut both the felt and lace following the scallops on lace.

3. Place lace on matching felt; pin together. Zigzag along edges to join.

4. Using open-toe foot, machine-appliqué along bottom (scalloped) edge twice using a medium-wide, slightly open zigzag stitch.

5. Using walking foot and a large stitch, machine-quilt layers together with a few wavy horizontal lines.

6. Repeat steps 3–5 for second half of hanger cover.

7. Place cover sections right sides facing. Sew halves together along top and sides, checking fit on your hanger and leaving a 3" opening in center top for inserting hanger hook.

8. Fold seam allowance to wrong side around opening; hand-stitch with needle and thread. Turn cover right side out; place on hanger.

Ribbon Rosette

1. Fold over raw edges on ends of 1½"-wide ribbon twice; stitch by hand.

2. Using double strand of quilting thread, sew a gathering stitch along one long edge, gathering ribbon tightly as you stitch and taking an occasional backstitch to hold gathers in place.

3. Roll gathered edge around itself, keeping gathered edges even and tacking layers to each other as you roll until entire rosette is secured.

4. Fold ³⁄₁₆"-wide ribbon in half; hand-stitch ribbon ends to folded-over end on back of flower. Hang rosette over hanger hook. ❧

*T*hese handy hangers pamper special garments with style! They make lovely shower and birthday gifts.

Fold

Lovely Lacy Hangers
Cut 2 on fold from felt
and 2 from scallop-edge lace

Cut along this edge to match scallops on lace

The simplest lotion, cologne or bath salt becomes glamorous when presented in this lovely container.

Decorative Boudoir Bottle

Design by Nancy Marshall

Project Note
Refer to photo throughout.

Instructions
1. Using stylus or toothpick, cover front surface of bottle with a pattern of diamonds formed with four dots of fuchsia paint. Let dry for several hours.

2. Using foam brush, cover painted surface with glaze; let dry.

3. Snip hanging loop off top of cupid charm; glue to bottle near top.

4. Wrap ribbon around neck of bottle; tie in bow in front.

5. Form a tiny bouquet of two roses, a leaf and a small sprig of baby's breath, twisting stems together. Hot-glue to one side of bottle neck under bow. Repeat to add a bouquet to other side. ❧

Materials
- 4" wide x 5" tall flat circular glass bottle
- Fuchsia PermEnamel satin-finish paint from Delta
- Delta Clear Gloss Glaze
- Toothpick or stylus
- Foam brush
- Gold-tone cupid charm from Creative Beginnings
- 12" piece ¼"-wide Colonial rose satin ribbon from Offray
- 4 pink paper roses
- Sprigs of silk baby's breath
- Wire cutters
- Hot-glue gun

**O**nce you've mastered the technique, you'll find it fun and easy to make cards of all styles, simply by varying the papers you choose.

Heart Frame Card

Design by Kathy Wegner

Materials

- 6½" x 5" Halcraft blank ivory greeting card with envelope
- Heart frame/flowers rubber stamp #K-222 (3¼" x 4¼") from Personal Stamp Exchange
- Black pigment ink pad
- Colored pencils: pink, red, green
- Decorative papers: 6½" x 5" blue/ecru stripe, 3" x 4" dusty pink plaid
- 4" x 5" ivory card stock
- 2" square woman's head from clip art
- PeelnStick double-sided adhesive sheets from Therm O Web
- Deckle paper edgers

Project Notes

Refer to photo throughout.

Follow manufacturer's instructions for using adhesive sheets.

Instructions

1. Ink rubber stamp; press onto ivory card stock. When dry, use colored pencils to color in flowers and leaves.

2. Apply adhesive sheets to back of striped and plaid papers, stamped design and woman's head. Using deckle edgers cut around stamped design. Using scissors cut out woman's head and heart opening in stamped design. Cut plaid to fit opening behind stamped design.

3. Peel off backing and apply as follows: press blue/ecru striped paper onto front of card; press woman's head onto plaid, and press plaid onto blue/ecru stripe; press stamped design over plaid, framing woman's head. ❀

Elegant Pearl Accessories

Designs by Marilyn Gossett

Materials

Ivy Pot

- 4½" x 4½" terra-cotta flowerpot
- 8 yards 3mm ivory pearls on string
- 1 yard 1"-wide green chiffon ribbon
- Floral foam to fit pot
- Ivy bush with 1"–1¾" varigated leaves
- 1" pink parchment rose
- 3 sprigs ¼" white silk baby's breath
- Dried green sheet moss
- Ivory #2036 Ceramcoat acrylic paint from Delta
- 1" flat paintbrush or small sea sponge

Each Bottle

- Decorative glass bottle with round wooden stopper
- 2 yards 3mm ivory pearls on string
- 16" 1"-wide green chiffon ribbon
- 1" pink parchment rose with 1" leaf
- 2 sprigs ¼" white silk baby's breath
- #12 flat paintbrush

Each Project

- Silver Renaissance Foil and adhesive from Delta
- Satin varnish sealer from Delta
- Tacky craft glue

Project Notes

Refer to photo throughout.

Follow manufacturer's instructions for applying foil and adhesive.

Ivy Pot

1. Paint pot inside and out with ivory paint; let dry.

2. Paint a band of glue around bottom of pot. Glue pearl string around bottom edge of pot, butting pearls up against each other and cutting off excess. Working from bottom to top, repeat until pot is covered with pearls.

3. Apply foil adhesive to rim of pot; let dry. Apply foil. Seal with varnish.

4. Tie ribbon around rim of pot; tie in a shoestring bow. Glue parchment rose and baby's breath in center of bow.

5. Place foam in pot. Arrange ivy bush in foam; place sheet moss around ivy to conceal foam.

Bottle

1. Paint a band of glue 1"–1¼" wide around bottom of bottle. Glue pearl string around bottom of bottle, cutting pearls so that they butt up against each other evenly. Repeat to add five more rows of pearls. Glue one more strand of pearls around neck of bottle.

2. Apply foil to stopper. Seal with varnish.

3. Tie ribbon around neck of bottle. Tie in a shoestring bow with 1½" loops and 2" tails; cut tails at an angle. Glue roses and baby's breath in center of bow. Insert stopper in bottle. ❁

Use these delightful designs as a spring-
board for your own ideas for classy accents.
How about pearl beads in pastel hues to match the guest bath?

Wedding Day Memory Book Page

Design by Judith Barker for
American Traditional Stencils

Materials

- Floral stencil #SP-651 from American Traditional Stencils
- Shiva Oil Stiks: naphthol red, Prussian blue, yellow ochre and sap green
- 4 (³⁄₁₆") stencil brushes
- ⅝" stencil brush
- Light table or sunny window
- Embossing tool
- Aleene's soft sand #OC 130 Premium-Coat acrylic paint
- Photo to fit in 2¾" x 4½" display area
- 8½" x 11" album page
- Masking tape
- Glue
- Sea sponge
- Waxed paper for palette

Create an heirloom memory page with favorite wedding snapshots!

Project Notes

Refer to photo throughout.

See directions for dry-brushing and stenciling under "Painting Techniques" in General Instructions on page 191.

Secure stencils with masking tape. Reduce tackiness of tape by applying it to your clothes a few times.

Though colors used on the sample are listed for each step, you can blend colors to create other shades. For a pastel effect, apply less color and lighter pressure.

When done with each stencil, carefully remove it and wipe clean.

Instructions

1. Rub some color from each oil stik onto waxed-paper palette. Apply yellow ochre to ⅝" brush; wipe off excess onto paper towel. Dry-brush color all over page to soften color and add texture.

2. Center stencil over page and tape in place. Placing tape over inside edges of rectangular cutout keeps paint off of space for photo.

3. To emboss, turn over album page onto light table. Rubbing your fingers over the paper allows the embossing tool to glide easily. Trace the outside edges of all design pieces. The weight of your paper will determine how much pressure will be needed to raise the design.

4. Turn page right side up. Stencil the pattern using a separate ³⁄₁₆" brush for each color. Generally speaking, on sample, flowers and buds are naphthol red shaded and highlighted with Prussian blue; leaves and vines are sap green and yellow ochre.

5. For corner designs, select a small portion of stencil pattern and tape over the surrounding unwanted spaces. Emboss, then stencil. Repeat in other corners.

6. Dab a barely damp sea sponge into a small puddle of soft sand paint; wipe off excess paint, then sponge very lightly all over page. Allow paint to dry thoroughly.

7. Place clean stencil over photo; using rectangular opening as a cropping guide, lightly mark photo where it should be trimmed. Trim photo, then apply glue to back of photo and glue in center of page. ❀

This ribbon-trimmed note card boasts all the sweetness of a Victorian nosegay.

Flower Basket Card

Design by Kathy Wegner

Materials

- Posh Impressions French Wire Basket rubber stamp from All Night Media
- Pigment pads: black, cocoa
- Card stock: 8½" x 11" pale green, 5½" x 4" ivory
- 2" x 3½" floral motif cut from art paper
- 4⅜" x 5¾" ivory envelope
- Fiskars Long Deckle paper edgers
- Fiskars ¼" flower paper punch
- Soft stencil brush
- Paper glue
- 25" 13mm pale green variegated silk ribbon

Project Note

Refer to photo throughout.

Instructions

1. Cut pale green card stock into two pieces, 5" x 6" and 5½" x 8".

2. Ink basket stamp with black; press onto center of 5" x 6" piece. Adhere floral motif over basket. Using deckle edgers, trim 5" x 6" card stock with flower basket to 3½" x 4¼".

3. Using stencil brush and cocoa ink, shade ivory card stock and edges of flower basket card stock. Using flower punch, punch flowers randomly over surface of ivory card stock.

4. Wrap ribbon lengthwise around punched ivory card stock; tie bow in front at center top. Glue flower basket card stock over ribbon on front of punched ivory card stock over bow ends.

5. Fold 5½" x 8" pale green card stock in half to make 5½" x 4" card; glue ivory card stock to front. ❀

Sweet Treat Pots

Designs by Mary Ayres

Materials

Each Container

- 6" clay flowerpot
- ½" round wooden furniture plug
- Popcorn yarn hair from Twice As Nice Designs Ltd.
- Americana acrylic paints from DecoArt: white wash #DA2, baby pink #DA31, lamp black #DA67, royal fuchsia #DA151, peony pink #DA215
- ZIG fine-tip black permanent marker from EK Success Ltd.
- Paintbrushes: #8 round bristle, #3 and #6 soft rounds
- Tacky craft glue
- Pinking paper edgers

Girl

- Fuchsia craft foam
- ⅝ yard ¾"-wide pink grosgrain ribbon
- ¼ yard 1"-wide pink satin ribbon with white polka dots
- 1 yard ⅜"-wide pink picot-edge satin ribbon
- Silk flowers: pink rosebud and baby's breath

Boy

- Pink craft foam
- ⅜ yard ⅝"-wide black satin ribbon
- ¾ yard 1½"-wide black satin ribbon

Project Notes

Refer to photo and pattern throughout.

Let paints and ink dry between applications.

For directions on transferring pattern, see "Using Transfer & Graphite Paper" in General Instructions, page 190.

See directions for dry-brushing and rouging under "Painting Techniques" in General Instructions, page 191.

Girl

1. Paint rim and inside of pot royal fuchsia. Paint remainder of pot and furniture plug (nose) baby pink.

2. Transfer eye, mouth and cheek details onto pot; bottom of mouth should be ¾" above bottom of pot. Paint pupils (tops of eyes) lamp black; paint heart cheeks peony pink; paint bottoms of eyes, tiny hearts in pupils and hearts in cheeks white wash. Rouge nose with peony

pink; dry-brush top edge of pot with white wash.

3. Using black marker, draw eye, mouth and cheek details. Glue nose to center of face where indicated by dot on pattern.

4. *Hatband:* Using pinking edgers, cut 8"-diameter circle from fuchsia craft foam. Using regular scissors, cut 5½"-diameter circle from center. Dry-brush pinked edges with white wash. Fit hatband over bottom of pot and push up to bottom of pot rim; glue under rim.

5. *Hair:* Lightly pencil a line around pot 1" below hat brim. Using one continuous length of yarn, glue yarn hair in vertical rows, filling 1" space all around pot.

6. Glue grosgrain ribbon around bottom of pot rim, overlapping ends at left front. Tie a knot in center of polka-dot ribbon; trim ends and glue knot over grosgrain ribbon ends. Glue rose and baby's breath on top of polka-dot

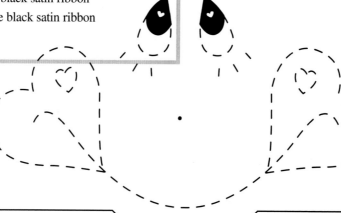

Sweet Treat Pots
Transfer collar onto
boy pot only

D ress up plain old flowerpots and they're nice enough to go anywhere, bearing Valentine's Day sweets, or presents for a new baby.

ribbon. Bend left front of hat brim downward; secure foam, flowers and ribbon in place with masking tape until glue is dry.

7. Wrap and glue picot-edge ribbon around bottom edge of pot, tying ends in a bow on right front.

8. Using scissors, cut 3¼"-diameter circle of craft

foam; glue to inside bottom of pot.

Boy

1. Transfer collar onto pot, extending line all the way around back of pot (top of collar should be 1⅝" up from bottom of pot). Paint collar and outside bottom of pot white wash; paint

remainder of pot and furniture plug (nose) baby pink.

2. Transfer face onto pot; paint and add details as in steps 2 and 3 for girl, adding collar details with black marker.

3. *Hair:* Using one continuous length of yarn, glue yarn hair in vertical rows all around rim of pot.

4. Glue ⅝" ribbon around bottom of pot rim, over-lapping ends at center front. Tie 1½" ribbon in a bow; trim ends and glue over ends of ⅝" ribbon.

5. Using scissors, cut 3¼"-diameter circle of craft foam; glue to inside bottom of pot. ❀

Celebrate Love • 79

"Quilted" Hearts Wall Hanging

Design by Kathy Wegner

Materials

- ½ yard 3-layer Warm & Natural quilted muslin
- Rainbow Felt Classic from Kunin: 5" x 10" each apricot, light yellow and teal; 5" square lavender
- Classic Impressions embossed felt from Kunin: 5" x 10" each antique white parquet, deep rose parquet, Wedgewood blue parquet, leaf green parquet, butterscotch snakeskin, canyon snakeskin
- Ivory 6-strand cotton embroidery floss and embroidery needle
- 15" ¼"-diameter wooden dowel
- 20" jute twine
- Pinking shears
- Fabric adhesive
- Pins

Embossed felt gives this colorful hanging all the texture of traditional quilting!

Project Notes

Refer to photo and pattern throughout.

Duplicate heart pattern; cut out and pin to felt before cutting.

Instructions

1. Using pinking shears throughout, cut one heart from each color of felt *except* canyon snakeskin. Cut 4" square from each color of felt *except* lavender. Trim quilted muslin to 16" square.

2. Tack one heart to each square, using a drop of fabric adhesive in center: *top row, left to right*—deep rose heart to Wedgewood blue square, teal heart to butterscotch square, antique white heart to apricot square; *center row, left to right*—apricot heart to teal square, lavender heart to antique white square, light yellow heart to leaf green square; *bottom row, left to right*—leaf green heart to light yellow square, Wedgewood blue heart to canyon square and butterscotch heart to deep rose square.

3. Using 4 strands floss throughout, stitch hearts to squares with running stitch; stitch around edges of all squares with running stitch.

4. Affix felt hearts and squares to muslin square with fabric adhesive (quilted waves in muslin should run horizontally).

5. Glue dowel along top edge of hanging on wrong side. Tie knot in each end of jute; glue a knot in each upper corner on right side of hanging. Let adhesive cure completely before hanging. ✤

Heart
Cut 1 from each color felt
except canyon snakeskin

Wired Heart Card

Design by Kathy Wegner

Materials

- Wild Wire Deluxe Jig and Pegs Kit #3370
- Rose #3389 26-gauge wire from Wild Wire
- Wire cutters
- 4" x 6" white card stock
- 5" x 7" hot pink paper with white hearts
- 6½" x 5" blank white greeting card with envelope from Halcraft
- Fiskars Long Majestic paper edgers
- Paper glue or adhesive sheet
- Invisible thread and slender needle

Project Note

Refer to photo and diagrams throughout.

Instructions

1. Referring to Fig. 1, position medium pegs at A and D and large pegs at B and C.

2. Cut four 12" pieces of wire. Holding wires together referring to Fig 2, loop centers around A. Wrap one set of wire ends around B and the other ends around C; ends meet under D. Twist wires twice under D; remove wire heart from jig.

3. Using paper edgers, cut card stock to 3" x 5" and pink paper to 4" x 6". Using thread and needle, tack wire heart to center of card stock in several places.

4. Glue pink paper to center of card front; glue card stock with wire heart to center of pink paper. ❀

Wrap wild-colored wires around pegs to make a bright, flashy heart, then affix it as the centerpiece on a unique greeting card.

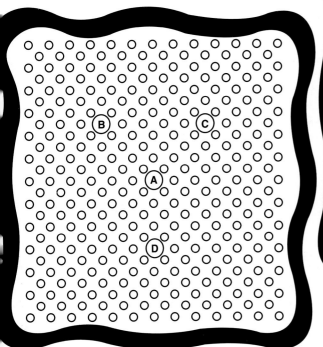

Fig. 1
Position pegs

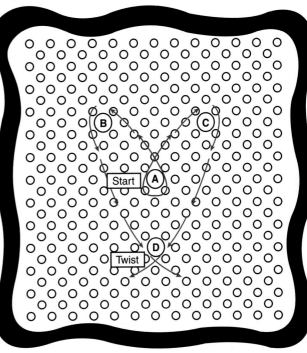

Fig. 2
Wrap wires around pegs

Winged Fairy Trinket Box continued from page 66

red-pearl mixture used on wings; shade right edge of bow and edges of dress with a little undiluted tompte red.

6. Paint skin fleshtone; shade with a mixture of equal parts 14K gold and fleshtone. Paint hair spice brown; highlight with undiluted 14K gold. Add a tiny dot of undiluted spice

brown for eye. Paint collar with pearl luster to which a touch of tompte red has been added. Paint arrow with undiluted 14K gold.

7. Using small needle and very fine (#4) gold braid, "sew" a bowstring onto bow, securing ends of braid on back with hot glue.

8. Go over transferred outlines and redefine details

with a sharp lead pencil.

9. To give wings extra dimension, carefully cut *between wings* from top down to point where wings meet fairy's arm. Slide tab of wings into slit and hot-glue in place.

Painting Box & Finishing

1. Paint exterior of box and rim of lid with tompte

red to which a little pearl luster has been added.

2. Glue fairy panel to top of lid. Conceal edge by gluing on a band of flat gold braid, beginning and ending behind wings.

3. Glue ribbon rosettes to fairy's hair. ❀

Stenciled Pajamas

Designs by Phyllis Sandford

Materials

- Pink cotton or cotton-blend T-shirt
- Off-white cotton or cotton-blend knit pants
- PermEnamel Heart to Hand stencil from Delta
- Stencil Magic Paint Cremes from Delta: charcoal green #90132, black cherry #90137, raspberry pink #90143, copper #90203
- Stencil Magic adhesive spray from Delta
- Stencil brushes: ⅜" and 3 (¼")
- Masking tape

Cuddle up with your beloved in these pretty stenciled "jammies" fashioned from a comfy cotton T-shirt and knit pants. Ooh-la-la!

Project Note

Use a different brush for each color paint. Refer to photo and patterns throughout.

Instructions

1. Prewash T-shirt and pants without using fabric softener; dry.

2. Following instructions on can, spray adhesive on back of stencil.

3. Place heart stencil on shirt under center of neckline according to pajamas top pattern. Open stencil paints and peel away puddinglike skin.

4. Holding ⅜" brush straight up and down, pounce end of the brush into black cherry paint. Work brush back and forth across a paper towel so there is just a little paint left on brush.

5. Place end of stencil brush on heart stencil and, using a circular motion, move over onto fabric off the stencil. Remember to hold brush straight up and down as you stencil in a circular motion. Leave some of the pink shirt showing through as a highlight and darken the left side of the heart by stenciling longer on the left side.

6. Using ¼" brush and raspberry pink, stencil design over heart.

7. Using charcoal green and ¼" brush, stencil design under heart.

8. Using copper and ¼" brush, stencil design between hearts.

9. Using same technique and colors, stencil sleeves using pajamas sleeve pattern and hem of shirt using pajamas hem pattern.

10. Stencil pajama pants using pajamas leg pattern, repeating pattern sections and staggering them about 4" apart down left leg.

11. Stencil right leg and backs of legs in the same manner with small design only, using copper.

12. Stencil around hem of pants legs using only charcoal green and bottom portion of the heart pattern; cut a piece of tape to mask the bottom of the heart shape so no charcoal green paint gets in the heart design.

13. Let the paint dry for at least 10 days before washing. It does not need to be heat-set. Wash in cool water. Clean brushes and stencils thoroughly with soap and warm water; for stubborn paints, use mineral spirits. ❀

Middle

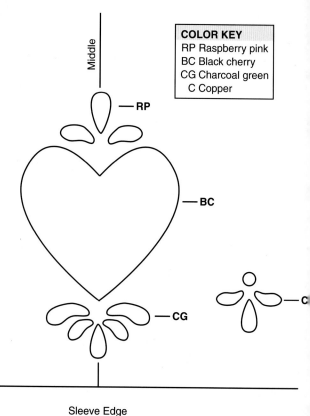

COLOR KEY
RP Raspberry pink
BC Black cherry
CG Charcoal green
C Copper

— RP

— BC

— CG

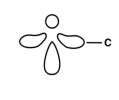

— C

— C

Sleeve Edge

Stenciled Pajamas Sleeve

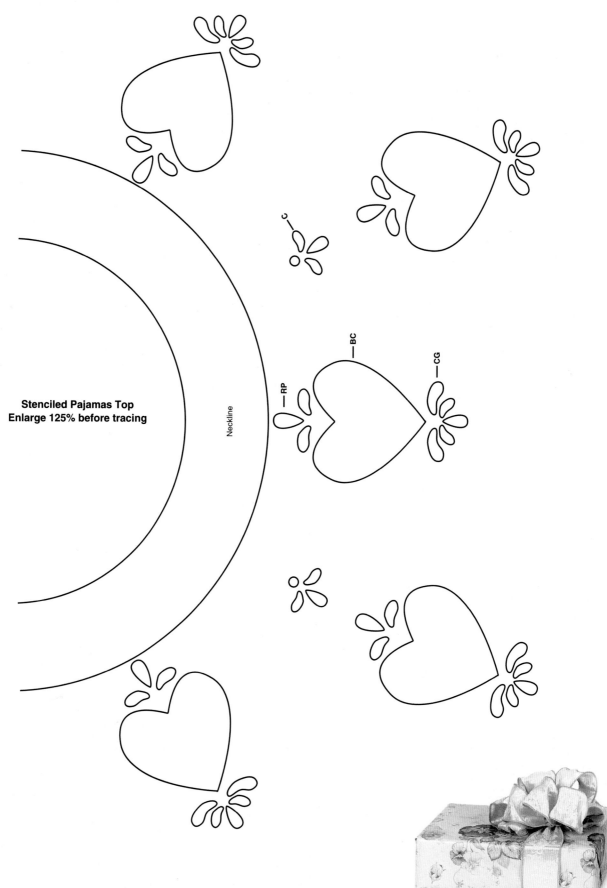

Stenciled Pajamas Top
Enlarge 125% before tracing

Neckline

C

RP

BC

CG

— C

COLOR KEY
RP Raspberry pink
BC Black cherry
CG Charcoal green
 C Copper

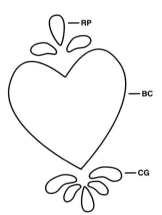
— RP
— BC
— CG

Stenciled Pajamas Leg
Enlarge 125% before tracing

— RP
— CG

Hem Stitching Line

Bottom of Shirt

Stenciled Pajamas Hem
Enlarge 125% before tracing

Hugs & Kisses

elebrate the arrival of the newest family member with this collection of sweet gifts for Baby! Keepsake mementos as well as practical items will be treasured by the new parents. And, since all are easy to craft, you can create darling pieces for everyone you know having a baby!

Celestial Nursery Ornaments

Designs by Deborah Spofford

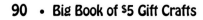

Materials

Block Ornament

- Walnut Hollow wooden products: 2" block, 1⅜" star, ¾" x 1½" primitive heart, 1" x 1⅛" moon
- Ceramcoat acrylic paints from Delta: pale yellow #2005, hydrangea pink #2449, white #2505, purple dusk #2522
- Coffee cup with swirl stamp #72059 from Rubber Stampede
- Stencil Buddy and stencil sponges from Delta
- Blue 20-gauge wire: 2 (15") pieces, 1 (21") piece
- Paintbrushes: #6 and #10 shaders, ⅝" glaze brush
- Round transparent plastic beads: 1 each purple, pink, yellow
- Acrylic gloss varnish from Delta
- Craft drill and 1/16" bit
- Needle-nose wire cutters
- 150-grit sandpaper
- Tack cloth
- Wood glue

Angel

- Wooden small garden angel #12884 from Walnut Hollow
- Ceramcoat acrylic paints from Delta: apple green #2065, white #2505, purple dusk #2522, mello yellow #2553
- Swirl heart stamp #72147 from Rubber Stampede
- Stencil Buddy and stencil sponges from Delta
- 6 swirl hair accessories from Darcie
- ⅝" glaze paintbrush
- Fine-point black permanent marking pen
- Acrylic gloss varnish from Delta
- 20" ¼"-wide off-white picot-edge satin ribbon
- Hot-glue gun
- Picture hanger

Project Notes

Refer to photo throughout.

Using paint on rubber stamps: For best results, apply paint to stamp with a stencil sponge. Dip sponge in paint and then pat paint onto stamp. This helps control the amount of paint on the stamp.

Let all coats of paint, varnish and ink dry between applications.

Block Ornament

1. Drill hole from front to back through bottom of each wooden ornament. Lightly sketch a ¾" triangle in center of block on top; drill a hole straight down at each point of triangle. Sand over holes; wipe off dust with tack cloth.

2. Using shaders, paint all surfaces of block and star purple dusk. Paint moon pale yellow and heart hydrangea pink.

3. Apply hydrangea pink to swirl on coffee cup stamp; stamp each side of block with swirl, reapplying paint to swirl between each stamp.

4. Cut ½" cube of stencil sponge and place in Stencil Buddy. Dip sponge in white paint; tap on paper towel to remove some of the paint and evenly distribute it across sponge. Rub sponge along all edges of block, star, heart and moon.

5. Using glaze brush, coat each piece with varnish, keeping holes open.

6. Curl wires randomly and unevenly around pencil, leaving ¾" straight at each end. Longest piece of wire should curl to about 5".

7. Slip straight end of wire through hole in star; twist to hold star upright. Repeat with remaining wires, moon and heart.

8. Apply small amount of wood glue to remaining straight end of star wire; slip on a bead and slide wire end into hole at top of triangle on block. Glue moon and heart wires with remaining beads in remaining holes.

9. When glue is dry, adjust wires, using needle-nose wire cutters to pinch or spread curls as desired.

Angel

1. Paint angel body purple dusk; paint wings mello yellow.

2. Apply apple green paint to heart stamp. Stamp heart on bottom of angel's skirt.

3. Cut ½" cube of stencil sponge; place in Stencil Buddy. Dip sponge in white paint; tap on paper towel to remove some of the paint and evenly distribute it across sponge. Rub sponge along edges of angel and wings to give them a slightly worn look. Dot on eyes with black marker.

4. Coat angel and wings with varnish.

5. Hot-glue swirls around angel's head.

6. Tie ribbon around angel's neck in a bow.

7. Hot-glue picture hanger to back of angel. ❀

Give the nursery a dash of color with this whimsical duo, including a gentle guardian angel with really funky hair and a coordinating wooden block ornament.

Beribboned Gift Boxes

Design by Mary Ayres

Materials

Each Box

- 2½" x 3½" papier-mâché box with lid from D&CC
- ⅝ yard ⅞"-wide sheer white wired ribbon
- 1" white ribbon flower from Offray
- Americana acrylic paint from DecoArt: baby blue #DA42 or petal pink #DA214
- Dazzling Metallics pearl paint from DecoArt: sky blue pearl #DA121 or rose pearl #DA119
- #8 round bristle paintbrush
- Tacky craft glue

Project Notes

Refer to photo throughout.

Let paints dry between applications.

Blue Box

1. Paint outside of box and lid with two coats baby blue paint.

2. Paint outside of box and lid with one coat sky blue pearl paint.

3. Cut two 10" pieces of ribbon. Glue one end of each piece to center of lid's short side on inside of lid. Let glue dry thoroughly.

4. Tie ribbon ends in a bow on center top of box lid. Trim ribbon ends evenly and shape bow. Glue flower in center of bow.

Pink Box

1. Paint outside of box and lid with two coats petal pink paint.

2. Paint outside of box and lid with one coat rose pearl paint.

3. Cut two 10" pieces of ribbon. Glue one end of each piece to inside of lid's long side, slightly off-center, with ribbons lining up across from each other. Let glue dry thoroughly.

4. Tie ribbon ends in a bow across top of box lid. Trim ribbon ends evenly and shape bow. Glue flower in center of bow. ❦

Present tiny tokens of love in these stylish little boxes!

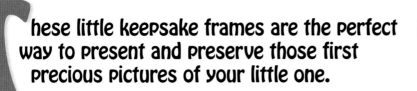

These little keepsake frames are the perfect way to present and preserve those first precious pictures of your little one.

Project Note
Refer to photo throughout.

Large Blue Frame
1. Using ruler and pencil, draw horizontal and vertical lines ¼" apart on frame front. Draw a dot with blue marker at every other intersection. Erase pencil lines.

2. Using ruler and blue marker, draw diagonal lines running from dot to dot and reversing slant of line in every other square to make a diamond shape.

3. Glue blue braid trim around outer edges of frame, beginning and ending at center top. Glue trim around edges of frame opening, beginning and ending at center bottom.

4. Glue blue bow at center top of frame's outer edge and at center bottom of frame opening edge to conceal ends of braid trim. Let dry.

Small Pink Frame
Repeat procedure for making large blue frame, using smaller frame, salmon marker and pink trim and bows instead of blue. ❧

Ribbon-Trimmed Frames

Design by Mary Ayres

Materials
Both Frames

- Pop-Up Paper frames: 4" x 5" and 6" x 7½"
- ZIG Memory System fine-tip permanent writers from EK Success Ltd.: blue and salmon
- 1" ribbon bows with pearl centers from Offray: 2 each blue and pink
- ¼" braid trim from Carolace: 1 yard pink and 1½ yards blue
- Tacky craft glue

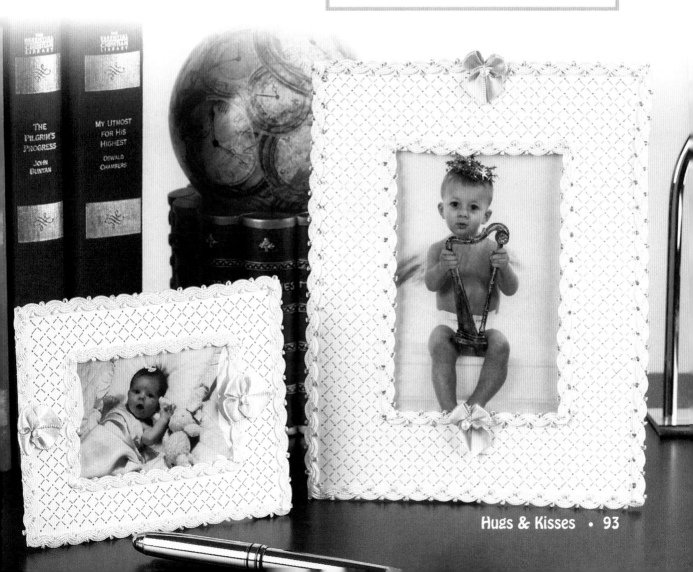

Sweet Breezes Bibs

Designs by Mary Ayres

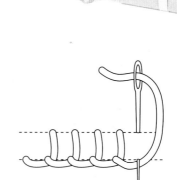

Materials

Sunny Bib

- 8" white square bib with crochet edging from Wimpole Street Creations
- 3"-diameter round white Battenburg doily
- Cadmium yellow #DA10 Americana acrylic paint from DecoArt
- ⅜"-diameter flat round yellow button
- Embroidery floss: yellow, orange
- Embroidery and hand-sewing needles

Flower Bib

- 8" white round bib with crochet edging from Wimpole Street Creations
- 3 (2"-diameter) round white Battenburg doilies
- Americana acrylic paints from DecoArt: spice pink #DA30, olive green #DA56
- ⅜"-diameter flat round turquoise button
- Embroidery floss: olive green, turquoise, pink
- Embroidery and hand-sewing needles

Blanket Stitch

Stem Stitch

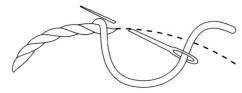

Project Notes

Refer to photo and diagrams for blanket stitch and stem stitch throughout.

To dye doilies: Mix 1 capful paint with 4 capfuls water in bowl. Saturate doily in mixture. Using your hands, wring out as much paint mixture as possible. Smooth doily flat and air-dry right side up on paper towels. When dry, press with iron between two pieces of paper. Once doily is completely dry, color is permanent and will not run.

Use 3 strands embroidery floss for all embroidery and attaching buttons.

Sunny Bib

1. Dye doily using cadmium yellow paint as described in Project Notes.

2. Pin doily in center of bib. Using 1 strand yellow floss, sew doily to bib around edges using tiny invisible stitches.

3. Using orange floss, embroider around center of doily with blanket stitch so that loops point outward. Using yellow floss, stem stitch rays coming from sun.

4. Sew yellow button to center of sun using orange floss.

Flower Bib

1. Dye one doily using spice pink paint and two using olive green paint as described in Project Notes.

2. Fold olive green doilies (leaves) in half, wrong sides facing. Pin doilies to bib. Using 1 strand olive green floss, sew doilies to bib around edges using tiny invisible stitches.

3. Using turquoise floss, embroider around centers of leaf doilies with blan-ket stitch so that loops point outward.

4. Pin spice pink doily to bib. Using 1 strand pink floss, sew doily to bib around edges, using tiny invisible stitches.

5. Using turquoise floss, embroider around center of doily with blanket stitch so that loops point outward.

6. Sew turquoise button to center of flower using pink floss. ❀

Tiny doilies are the secrets to these lovely bibs. They look lovely on dollies and teddy bears, too, so make one to match Baby's favorite.

Teddy Bear Puppet

Design by Kathy Wegner

Materials

- 9" x 18" Shaggy Plush Felt from Kunin (see Project Notes)
- 2" x 3" tan or brown suede
- ¼" round hole punch
- 2 (10mm) round black wiggle eyes (see Project Notes)
- Hot-glue gun
- Tacky craft glue

Project Notes

Refer to photo and patterns throughout.

Use any color of Shaggy Plush Felt you like; samples were made with bronzed copper and brown sugar.

For safety's sake, consider replacing the wiggle eyes with sewn-on eyes made of black and white felt if puppet will be used by a very young child.

Instructions

1. Cut two bears from folded felt, aligning pattern's dashed line with fold. Cut two paws and one nose from suede. Punch eight circles from suede for "toes."

2. Unfold bears; glue them together wrong sides facing, carefully running a bead of hot glue around edges; leave bottom open.

3. Using tacky glue, glue nose and eyes to bear's face; glue suede paws and toes in place. Let dry completely. ✿

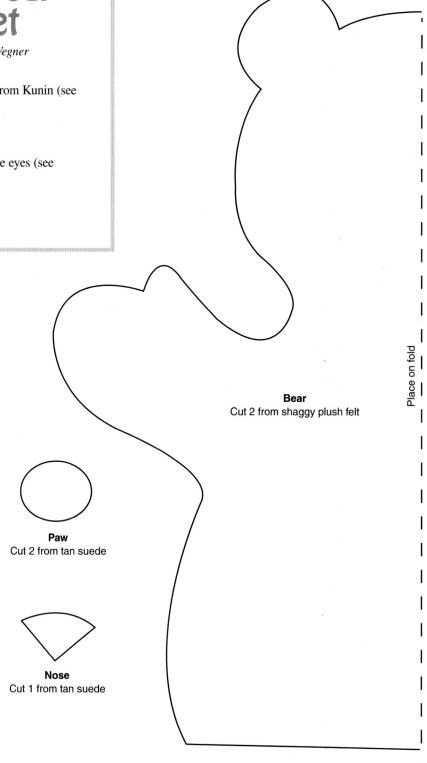

Bear
Cut 2 from shaggy plush felt

Place on fold

Paw
Cut 2 from tan suede

Nose
Cut 1 from tan suede

Puppets make outstanding playthings—
they encourage creativity and imagination.
This one is soft and cuddly, too!

The Tooth Fairy will have no problem finding what was "lost" when it's snuggled in one of these cute containers.

Tooth Fairy Treasure Boxes

Design by Chris Malone

Materials

Each Box

- 1¾" x 3" papier-mâché box with lid
- 2" wooden split doll pin
- Americana acrylic paint from DecoArt: sapphire #DA99 *or* peony pink #DA215, *plus* white wash #DA2, lamp black #DA67, base flesh #DA136, shading flesh #DA137
- Paintbrush
- Cotton-tip swab
- Toothpick
- Old toothbrush or spatter brush
- Black fine-line marking pen
- Krylon Matte Spray Finish
- Small piece mini-curl doll hair
- 1¼" x 2" piece blue or pink fabric in a tiny check or print
- Hand-sewing needle and thread to match fabric
- 6" piece ¹⁄₁₆"-wide white satin ribbon
- Seam sealant
- Craft adhesive

Project Notes

Refer to photo and pattern throughout.

Let paints, ink and spray finish dry between applications.

Blue Box

1. Paint box and lid inside and out with sapphire blue paint. Paint head of doll pin base flesh and bottom of doll white wash. Mix sapphire blue with white wash to make a paler shade and paint dress area of doll pin. Repaint all areas as necessary.

2. Paint white-wash wings on lid with top of wings ¾" from one short end of lid.

3. Thin white-wash paint with a little water. Dip bristles of toothbrush into mixture; holding brush 12" from box, pull thumb across bristles to spatter box and lid.

4. Dip cotton-tip swab in shading flesh; touch to doll face for cheeks. Dip toothpick in lamp black; touch to face for eyes.

5. Glue doll over wings on box lid. Spray box and lid with two coats matte finish.

6. Apply seam sealant to edges of fabric rectangle; let dry. Sew gathering stitches ⅛" from one long edge. Pull gathers until dress measures ¾" across; knot and clip thread. Glue gathered edge to doll's neck.

7. Tie ribbon in a tiny bow; trim ends at an angle. Glue bow to dress at neck.

8. Frizz doll hair between fingers; glue to top of head.

Pink Box

Follow instructions for blue box substituting peony pink for sapphire blue and pink fabric and thread for blue. ❀

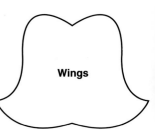

Wings

The hard part's done—these lightweight foam stars come complete with golden hanging loops, ready for decorating. Dress up presents for Baby, or make a sweet mobile!

Wish Upon a Star

Design by Samantha McNesby

Materials

Each Ornament

- Kreative Foam Star Ornament from Design A Line
- Stylus or dry ballpoint pen
- Acrylic paints: bright pink or bright blue *plus* metallic gold
- Small paintbrush

Project Note

Refer to photo throughout.

Instructions

1. Using pencil, lightly draw hearts or other designs on foam star. Using stylus or pen, scratch designs into the foam, using medium to firm pressure. Press point of pen firmly into foam to make dots between designs.

2. Paint all surfaces of foam star bright pink or blue. While paint is still wet, add streaks of gold, blending colors as desired. Let dry completely. ❅

Baby Stickers Gift Tin

Design by Nancy Marshall

Materials

- Tin box with lid (see Project Notes)
- Large and small stickers (see Project Notes)

Project Notes

Refer to photo throughout.

A 4"-wide, 3¼"-tall hexagonal white tin was used for the sample.

Choose stickers that will have either no background visible after they are peeled, or that have a background that complements your tin. The Frances Meyer ABC Train stickers used on the sample have a white background.

Instructions

1. Position a large sticker on each side of tin's base; "join" larger stickers as desired with smaller stickers (stars were used on sample project).

2. Arrange more small stickers around edge of lid as desired. ❅

Look for economical tins at party outlet stores and rummage sales to make cute catchalls!

Project Note

Refer to photo and patterns throughout.

Instructions

1. Cut dove from white felt, using scallop shears along wing and tail and regular scissors elsewhere. Using scissors, cut four each of stars A and B from light yellow.

2. Using wave shears throughout, cut 5" square misty blue, 7" square wave green and 9" square pink mist. Cut four ½" x 7" strips from pink mist.

3. Glue wave green square in center of pink mist square; glue misty blue square in center of wave green square. Glue dove in center of misty blue square. Glue stars together in matching pairs. Glue Stars A to upper left and bottom right corners of misty blue square; glue stars B to upper right and lower left corners.

4. Using needle and floss, sew ½" button in center of each star. Sew a ¾" button in each bottom corner of pink mist square. Hold two pink mist strips together but slightly off-center so that they cross slightly. Sew ends to top corner with another ¾" button; repeat on other top corner with remaining strips. Sew fifth ¾" button through strips where they cross at top center.

5. Outline dove with running stitch using white floss and needle.

6. Glue dowel along top back edge; let dry. ✿

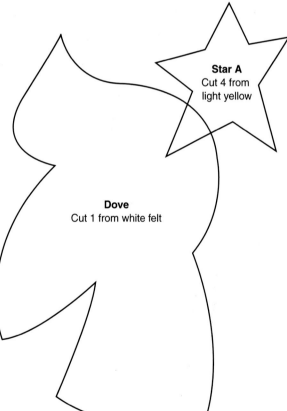

Star A
Cut 4 from light yellow

Dove
Cut 1 from white felt

Peaceful Dove

Design by Kathy Wegner

Materials

- Rainbow Felt Classics from Kunin: 9" x 12" each pink mist, wave green, misty blue, light yellow, white
- Softgrip scallop and wave shears from Fiskars
- White flat buttons: 4 (½"), 5 (¾")
- White 6-strand embroidery floss and embroidery needle
- Fabric adhesive
- 8½" wooden dowel or stick

Star B
Cut 4 from light yellow

hat a colorful and gentle design to add to your nursery! Hang it on the wall above the crib, or use it to decorate a door.

**N**ever worry about losing that treasured tooth before the Fairy can pay off! This little angel will keep it safe and sound!

Project Notes

Refer to photo throughout.

Let glue, primer, paints, ink and sealer dry between applications.

Instructions

1. Drill a hole straight down in top center (curved) edge of dome. Sand wooden pieces; wipe off dust with tack cloth. Using wood glue through step 2, glue ribbon banner to back of dome for wings.

2. Break off a small piece of toothpick that will fit in hole in dome and protrude a bit to fit in hole in bottom of ball knob. Glue into hole in dome. Glue ball knob (head) over other end.

3. Using foam brush, paint wood with primer. When dry, sand lightly and wipe with tack cloth.

4. Paint angel: *white*—

wings and mini pocketful; *blush*—ball knob head; *medium blue*—dome body; *medium yellow*—four stars. Give all pieces a second coat.

5. Using marker, dot eyes and draw smile on head; write "Deposit tooth here" on front of pocketful. Blush cheeks using cotton swab and ink pad. Squeeze swirls of beige 3-D paint onto head for hair. Squeeze dots of spa blue 3-D paint onto front of pocketful and wings; using toothpick, drag five points out from each to make stars.

6. Using craft cement, glue pocketful to front of angel so bottoms are flush; glue wooden stars to front of angel. When glue is completely cured, coat piece with matte varnish. ❁

Tooth Fairy Angel

Design by Kathy Wegner

Materials

- Darice Craftwood: 2⅞" x 2⅞" x ½" dome, 3½" x 1⅝" x ¼" ribbon banner, 1¼" ball knob, 4 (1" x ³⁄₁₆") pointed stars
- 2" x 1¼" x ⅞" wooden Mini Pocketful from Provo Craft (smallest from #11-2433 set of 3)
- Aleene's Enhancers: all-purpose primer #EN 104, matte varnish #EN 107
- Aleene's Premium-Coat acrylic paints: white #OC 173, blush #OC 183, medium blue #OC 150, medium yellow #OC 126
- Tulip Matte 3-D Paints: spa blue #65307, beige #65315
- Wood glue and heavy-duty craft cement
- Black fine-point permanent marking pen
- Pink pigment ink pad or cosmetic blush
- Craft drill with ⁵⁄₆₄" bit
- Sandpaper and tack cloth
- Round toothpicks
- Foam brush
- Paintbrush
- Cotton-tip swab

Fun for Kids

Whether looking for a way to spend some quality time with your kids, or simply to pass the hours on a rainy day, this collection of bright and colorful crafts is sure to please you and your youngsters! Decorated clothing, kids' gifts and much more will bring you hours of craft-time fun!

Groovy Gecko Cachepots

Designs by Samantha McNesby

Materials

Each Design

- Paintbrush
- Baking sheet
- Aluminum foil
- Toothpick

Mini Pot

- 2" terra-cotta flowerpot
- Sculpey III polymer clay: bright green, bright pink, black, white
- Acrylic paints: bright yellow, bright pink, bright orange, white

Pot With Lid

- 4" terra-cotta flowerpot with saucer
- 1" wooden ball knob
- 1" wooden disk
- Sculpey III polymer clay: bright yellow, hot pink, black, white
- Acrylic paints: bright yellow, bright pink, bright orange, white
- Bright pink dimensional fabric paint
- Foam brush
- Cotton-tip swab
- Thick craft glue
- Square toothpick or fork

Project Notes

Refer to photo throughout.

Let all coats of paint and glue dry between applications unless otherwise instructed.

Condition polymer clay before forming shapes by kneading it with your fingers until it is soft and pliable. Clean your hands often, especially when changing colors, to keep from contaminating one color with another.

Follow manufacturer's instructions for baking clay in oven.

Mini Pot

1. Paint pot white on all surfaces.

2. Paint interior of pot bright pink; paint rim bright orange; paint remainder of pot's exterior bright yellow.

3. *Lizard:* Roll 1" ball of bright green clay and form into a 3"-long snake, tapering one end to make tail. Pinch in about ½" from other end to form head. Press body onto side of pot, allowing the head to peek in over the edge. Roll four thin ¾"-long snakes for legs; attach legs to body by pressing them into place and smoothing out seams.

4. *Spots & Eyes:* Roll two ⅛" balls of white; press lightly to attach them to head. Roll two slightly smaller balls of black and press onto whites, allowing some white to show around black. Roll 17 (⅛") balls of bright pink clay and press onto lizard's back.

5. Bake entire pot and lizard on foil-covered baking sheet. Let cool completely.

6. Using toothpick dipped in white paint, add tiny highlight dot to pupil of each eye.

Variations

Purple Lizard: Paint interior of pot bright yellow, rim bright green and remainder of pot bright turquoise. Form lizard from purple polymer clay and add dots of royal blue clay.

Blue Lizard: Paint interior of pot bright turquoise, rim bright pink and remainder of pot bright green. Form lizard from royal blue polymer clay and add dots of light blue clay.

Pot With Lid

Painting

1. Paint all terra-cotta and wooden surfaces white using foam brush.

2. *Paint pot:* Paint interior bright pink; paint rim bright yellow; paint remainder of pot's exterior bright orange.

3. *Paint lid (saucer):* Paint interior of terra-cotta saucer bright yellow; paint rim and center bottom circle of saucer bright pink; paint remainder of saucer bright orange.

4. *Paint handle:* Paint ball knob bright yellow and wooden disk bright orange.

Modeling

1. *Lizard:* Roll 1½" ball of bright yellow clay and form into a 4"-long snake, tapering one end to make tail. Pinch in about 1" from other end to form head. Press body onto side of pot. Roll four slender 1"-long snakes from bright yellow clay for legs; attach legs to body by pressing them into place and smoothing seams.

2. *Eyes:* Roll two ¼" balls of white; press lightly to attach them to head. Roll two ⅛" balls of black and press onto whites, allowing some of white to show around black.

3. *Bug:* Roll two ½" balls of bright yellow clay for head and body; flatten each slightly. Roll two ⅜" balls of bright pink clay for wings; flatten and add crosshatching lines by pressing square toothpick

B

righten a dresser top, bathroom or desk with these colorful, whimsical catchalls! Use them to corral everything from paper clips to cotton balls!

or tine of fork lightly into surface. Press body onto surface of lid; press wings on top of body, positioning them off to sides slightly; press head over tips of wings. Add eyes to bug as in step 2, making them slightly smaller.

Baking & Finishing

1. Bake pot and lid on foil-covered baking sheet as directed. Let cool completely before handling.

2. Using cotton-tip swab dipped in bright yellow paint, add spots randomly to orange surface of pot. Using small brush, paint vertical bright yellow stripes on bright pink rim of lid.

3. Using bright pink dimensional paint throughout, add a spot atop each yellow dot; add spots to lizard, and dots at ends of legs for toes; add spots to surface of yellow ball knob.

4. Using toothpick dipped in white paint, add tiny highlight dot to pupil of each eye.

5. Glue orange disk to center of lid; glue yellow ball knob in center of orange disk. Let glue cure completely before handling.

Variations

Blue Lizard

Paint interior of pot bright turquoise, rim royal blue and remainder of pot lime green. Paint interior of lid bright green, center bottom circle royal blue, rim in

stripes of lime green and royal blue, bottom center circle with royal blue, and remainder of lid bright turquoise.

Substitute wooden star cutout for disk; paint star lime green and ball knob bright turquoise.

Form lizard from turquoise polymer clay; form bug using neon green for body, royal blue for wings and turquoise for head.

After baking, use cotton swab to dot pot with turquoise glitter paint;

top with dots of bright green dimensional paint. Use bright green dimensional paint to add spots and toes to lizard and spots to ball knob.

Pink Lizard

Paint interior of pot bright pink, rim bright green and remainder of pot bright yellow. Paint interior of lid bright yellow, center bottom circle bright green, rim in stripes of lime green and bright yellow, and remainder of lid bright pink. Paint disk

bright yellow and ball knob bright pink. Form lizard from hot pink polymer clay; form bug using bright yellow for body, neon green for wings and hot pink for head.

After baking, use cotton swab to dot pot with bright pink paint; top with dots of bright green dimensional paint. Use bright green dimensional paint to add spots and toes to lizard and spots to ball knob. ❧

Bee Buddy

Design by Carolyn V. Stearns

Materials

- Miniature bottle gourd, approximately 4" tall and 2½" in diameter
- Laundry bleach
- Copper scrub pad
- ¼"-diameter wooden dowel
- 2 (⁵⁄₁₆") round wooden plugs
- Kunin Kreative Kanvas
- 2 (1½") wooden half-eggs
- 2 (⁵⁄₃₂") black beads
- 12" ⅛"-wide yellow satin ribbon
- Toner Plastic 24-gauge Fun Wire: licorice, icy gold, candy apple
- Krylon aerosol products: Spray Gesso and Crystal Clear
- ZIG 05 black Millennium Marker from EK Success Ltd.
- Craft cement
- Americana acrylic paints from DecoArt: white wash #DA2, cadmium yellow #DA10, boysenberry pink #DA29, lamp black #DA67, Santa red #DA170
- Shimmering silver #DA70 Dazzling Metallics paint from DecoArt
- DecoArt Glamour Dust #DAS37
- Paintbrushes: #0 liner, #1 round, #12 shader
- Stylus
- Craft saw
- Drill with ¹⁄₁₆" and ⁵⁄₁₆" bits

Project Notes

Refer to photo, Fig. 1 and patterns throughout.

See instructions for dry-brushing and base-coating under "Painting Techniques" in the General Instructions on page 191.

Let all coats of gesso, paint, ink and finish dry between applications unless instructed otherwise.

Bee

1. Using copper scrub pad and ¼ cup bleach mixed with warm water, clean gourd thoroughly, making sure gourd is smooth and free of dirt and debris. Dry thoroughly.

2. Spray gourd with gesso.

3. Drill two ⁵⁄₁₆" holes in bottom (blossom) end of gourd, one hole on each side of blossom stub.

4. Insert ¼" dowel in one hole as far as it will go, being careful not to push dowel through top or side of gourd. When dowel is in place, measure 3" of dowel protruding from gourd and mark; remove dowel and cut at this mark. Repeat to make second leg.

5. *Face:* Draw face on upper portion of gourd. (Gourds will vary in shape and proportion, so use Fig. 1 as a general guide.) Paint face white wash; dry-brush cheeks with boysenberry pink. Paint nose boysenberry pink. Dot on two tiny lamp black eyes and add tiny, tiny white wash eye highlights. Paint mouth lamp black. Add white wash comma stroke to nose and mouth, and highlight dots to cheeks.

6. Paint remainder of gourd lamp black. Beginning at neck, measure and outline three stripes around bee. Base-coat stripes with white wash, then paint with cadmium yellow, using two coats if necessary.

7. *Shoes:* Drill a ⁵⁄₁₆" hole down into rounded end of each wooden half-egg; paint shoes Santa red on all surfaces.

8. *Legs:* Reinsert dowel legs into bottom of gourd. Glue wooden plug "knee" to each leg 1" below gourd. Paint legs and knees lamp black. Insert ends of dowels into shoes and adjust position so bee will stand.

9. Spray bee with two or three coats of Crystal Clear.

Wings & Final Assembly

1. Cut two wings, reversing one, from canvas. Dry-brush wings with shimmering silver to give a mottled effect. Spray with Crystal Clear, and while finish is still wet, add a small amount of Glamour Dust on wings. Repeat on other side.

2. Using marker, add dot-dash outline around wings on front.

3. Using craft saw or other sharp edge, make shallow 1⅛"-long cuts on sides for wings; apply a little glue to edges of wings and insert in slits.

4. *Antennae:* Drill two ¹⁄₁₆" holes in top of head. Cut two 2" pieces licorice wire; coil around paintbrush. Put a bead on one end of each piece and twist wires so beads stay in place. Glue other ends of wires in holes.

5. Cut two 6" pieces red wire and two 6" pieces gold. Twist one wire of each color around each ankle, coiling wire ends around round paintbrush handle. Trim wire ends and arrange as desired.

6. Tie ribbon in a bow around bee's neck. ❀

Growing gourds is a great project for kids—and the crop makes great crafts for creative little fingers, such as this friendly bumblebee!

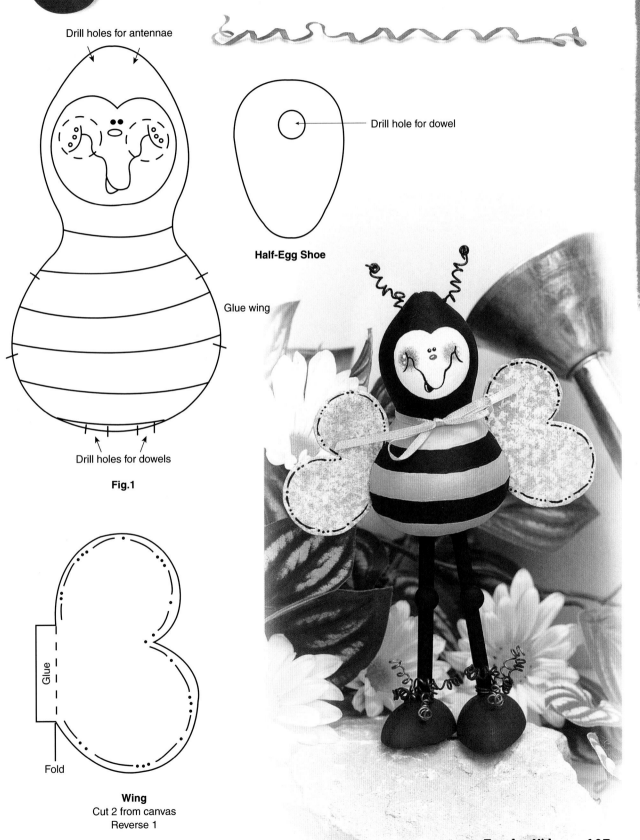

Drill holes for antennae

Drill hole for dowel

Half-Egg Shoe

Glue wing

Drill holes for dowels

Fig.1

Glue

Fold

Wing
Cut 2 from canvas
Reverse 1

Project Note

Refer to photo and pattern (page 110) throughout.

Gift Sack

1. Using blue jay marker, write "PARTY PARTY PARTY" down front of sack. Add swirls with rose marker, clusters of three dots with apricot marker, and dashes with spring green marker.

2. Outline/highlight letters and details with black marker.

"Let's Party" T-Shirt

1. Place T-shirt painting board inside T-shirt. Slide T-shirt pattern between painting board and T-shirt; outline pattern on shirt with water-soluble marker.

2. Paint "Let's Party" true blue. Apply bright red paint to swirl sponge and stamp small swirls onto shirt as desired. Using the end of paintbrush handle, add random clusters of three yellow dots. Add spring green dashes.

3. Outline/highlight painted designs with black marker.

4. Heat iron to hot setting, no steam. Place waxed paper over painted area and iron over design for approximately two minutes to heat-set paint. ✿

"Let's Party!" Gift Sack & T-Shirt

Designs by Paula Bales

Materials

Gift Sack

- 5¼" x 8½" white paper sack
- ZIG Memory System 1.2mm writers from EK Success Ltd.: blue jay, apricot, rose, spring green
- ZIG Memory System 05 black Millennium marker from EK Success Ltd.
- Stylus

T-Shirt

- Child's white T-shirt
- Water-soluble marker
- Apple Barrel acrylic paints from Plaid: spring green, yellow, bright red, true blue
- Paintbrushes: #2 and #10 shaders
- Small swirl Fun to Paint Sponge from Plaid
- Stylus or pin with round head
- ZIG Memory System 08 black Millennium marker
- T-shirt painting board
- Iron
- Waxed paper

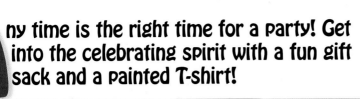

Any time is the right time for a party! Get into the celebrating spirit with a fun gift sack and a painted T-shirt!

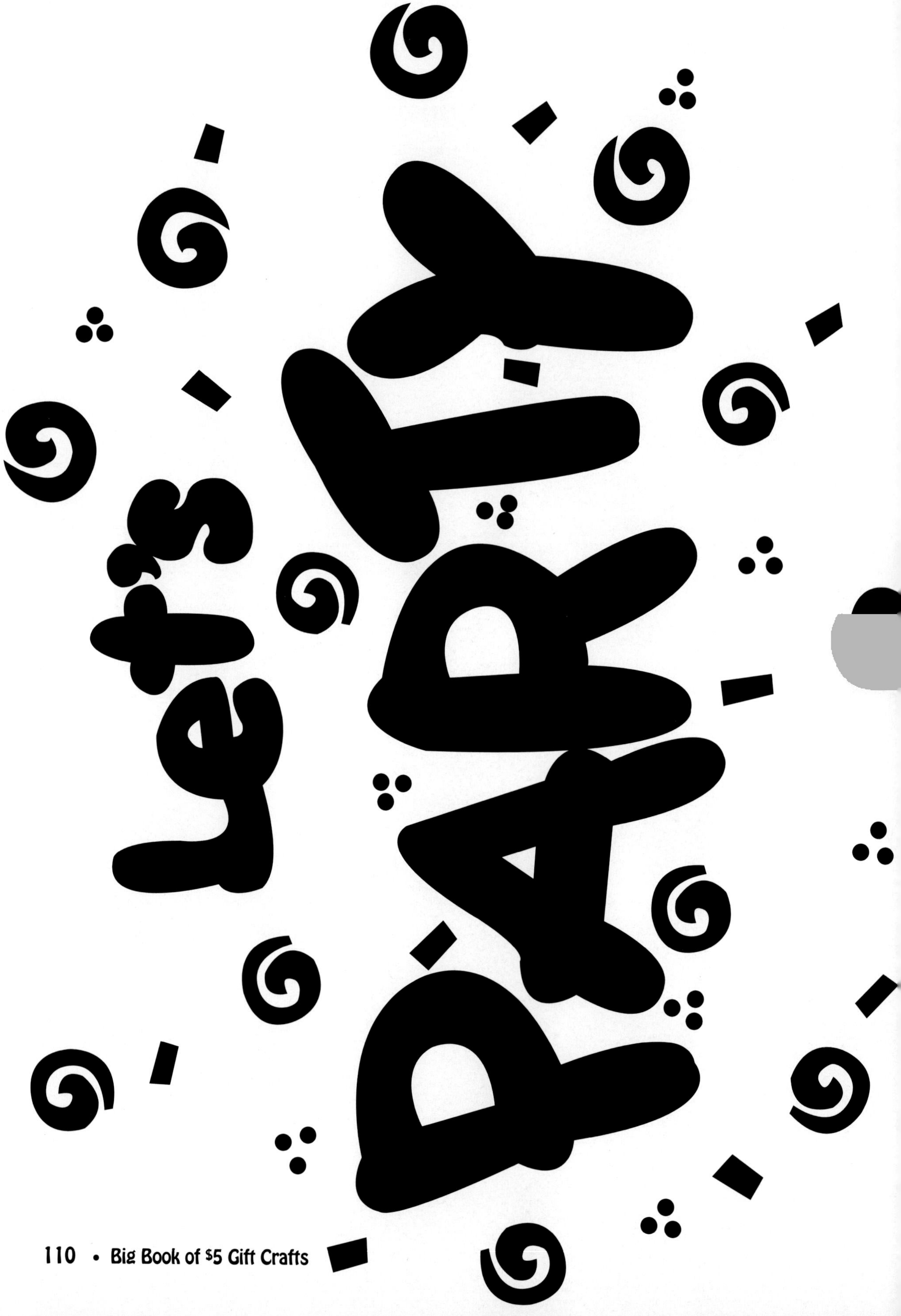
Let's
PARTY

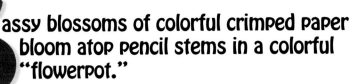

Sassy blossoms of colorful crimped paper bloom atop pencil stems in a colorful "flowerpot."

Blooming Daisies Pencils

Design by Deborah Spofford

Materials

- 5 new yellow pencils
- 4½"-tall soup can, cleaned, dried, with label and one end removed
- 5 bright green chenille stems
- Fiskars 65-lb. card stock: 1 sheet each purple and bright green; 3" square each blue, yellow, orange and pink
- ½" pompoms: green, yellow, fuchsia, 2 orange
- ¾" pompoms: purple, orange, fuchsia, yellow
- Fiskars paper crimper and Victorian paper edgers
- Hot-glue gun

Project Note

Refer to photo and pattern throughout.

Instructions

1. Cut flowers from card stock: four bright green, one each blue, orange, pink, purple and yellow. Run each through paper crimper.

2. Glue ¾" pompoms to centers of green flowers.

Glue ½" pompoms to centers of other flowers: orange pompom to yellow flower, fuchsia pompom to blue flower, orange pompom to purple flower, yellow pompom to pink flower and green pompom to orange flower.

3. Cut purple card stock 6½" x 11½"; run through crimper. Wrap crimped card stock around can (so crimps run vertically) and align bottom edge of card stock with bottom edge of can. Glue ends of card stock where they overlap; carefully fold top of card stock to inside of can smoothly and glue.

4. Using paper edgers, cut two 11" x ¼" strips green card stock; run through crimper. Glue strips around can, ½" below top and ½" above bottom.

5. Wrap a chenille stem around each pencil; secure with glue as needed. Glue purple, pink, orange, blue and yellow flowers to eraser ends of pencils. Glue green flowers around center of can, spacing them evenly. Insert pencils in can. ❁

Blooming Daisies
Cut 4 from bright green card stock and 1 each from yellow, blue, orange, pink and purple

Mini Frame

Design by Samantha McNesby

Materials

- Coordinating fabric scraps at least 4" square of 2 coordinating fabrics, plus 2" square of 1 of the fabrics
- Batting at least 6" square
- 2 scraps cardboard or mat board at least 3" square
- Thick craft glue
- Small magnet

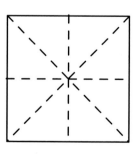

Back
Cut 1 from cardboard
and 1 from batting

Next time you send the latest school photo to Grandma, enclose it in this sweet frame with a magnet on the back!

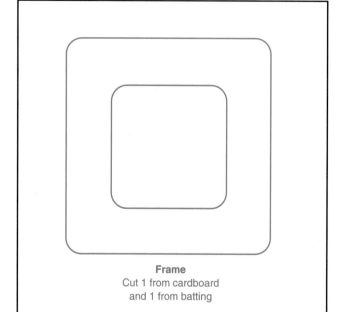

Frame
Cut 1 from cardboard
and 1 from batting

Frame Backing
Cut 1 from fabric

Frame Front
Cut 1 from fabric
Snip fabric in opening
along dotted lines

Preserve your star's moment in the spotlight with this colorful, simple frame. It's the perfect size for a "sports card" featuring your star, or a school photo.

All-Star Frame

Design by Reba Campbell

Materials

- 5" x 6" wooden frame with 2" x 3" opening from Lara's Crafts
- Woodsies wooden stars from Forster: 3 medium, 2 large
- Americana acrylic paints from DecoArt: primary yellow #DA201, admiral blue #DA213
- ½" paintbrush
- ZIG 01 pure black Millennium marker from EK Success Ltd.
- Thick craft glue
- Masking tape
- Clear matte sealer
- Ribbon, twine, sawtooth hanger, magnet strip (optional)

Project Notes

Refer to photo throughout.

Let paints, ink and sealer dry between applications.

Instructions

1. Paint all surfaces of frame admiral blue; paint fronts and edges of stars primary yellow. *Note: Use masking tape to help hold stars while painting them.*

2. Using marker, outline stars with dot-dot-dot-dash pattern; glue stars to frame.

3. Using tip of paintbrush handle dipped in primary yellow, dot on rows of "stardust" trailing each star.

4. Spray frame with sealer.

5. Attach photo to back of frame with tape. Add twine, ribbon, sawtooth hanger or magnet strip to back of frame as desired. ✿

Mini Frame

Project Note

Refer to photo and patterns throughout.

Instructions

1. From cardboard, cut one frame and one back.

2. From batting, cut one frame and one back.

3. Cut one frame front from one fabric scrap, carefully clipping center opening along dotted lines; cut one frame backing from the other.

4. Glue batting frame to cardboard frame and batting back to cardboard back; let dry.

5. Lay frame batting side up; top with fabric frame front. Fold excess fabric to back of frame and glue. Repeat with fabric frame backing and batting/card-board back.

6. Trim photo to fit opening in frame. Center photo on top of fabric-covered back; glue frame on top.

7. Cut 2" square of fabric to cover back of frame, folding under raw edges to fit. Glue magnet to back of frame. ✿

Apples for Teacher

Design by Bonnie Lester

Materials

- 12-ounce glass mug
- Black Liquid Leading from Plaid
- Gallery Glass window colors from Plaid: cameo ivory #16003, kelly green #16008, ruby red #16015
- Plastic sheet protector or glass from a picture frame
- Large paper clip

Project Notes

Refer to photo and patterns throughout.

Rinsing of interior only is recommended if mug is to be used for drinking.

Refer to manufacturer's instructions for using leading and window colors. Where leading spreads too wide or runs together, let it stand for 5–10 minutes, then gently reshape with a toothpick.

Applying Leading

1. Place glass or sheet protector directly over pattern. Poke hole in tip of liquid leading bottle using a large paper clip.

2. Holding bottle vertically and applying firm, even pressure, go over pattern outlines, making two sets of leaves. For optimal control, grasp bottle as if you were holding a broomstick. Keeping bottle tip above work, allow an even "rope" of leading to fall in place over pattern lines. To end a line, gently touch tip to glass and release pressure on bottle at the same time.

3. *Seeds:* Touch tip of leading bottle to glass at wide end of seed; squeeze a small dot of leading out of bottle and move tip toward narrow end of seed, releasing pressure at the same time.

4. Set aside leading to dry completely—about 24 hours, depending on heat and humidity.

Applying Colors

1. First squeeze a line of color along inside of leaded outlines; this prevents color from shrinking away from outline as it dries.

2. Using even pressure, fill remaining areas with a generous amount of glass paint by moving the tip back and forth, as if coloring a picture. Use ruby red for the whole apples, kelly green for the leaves and cameo ivory and ruby red for the apple slices.

3. Tap underside of project to raise most of the bubbles to the top, then gently comb through colored areas with a toothpick, popping bubbles as necessary. It helps to keep the end of the toothpick very dry.

4. Set aside painted designs to dry completely—about 24 hours, depending on heat and humidity. Colors are translucent and no longer cloudy when dry.

Finishing

Gently peel leaves and apples from glass and arrange on mug as desired. Allow seven days to cure. Keep in mind that filling the mug with hot or cold liquid could cause the painted designs to slip or soften. ❀

Patterns continued on page 117

Single Apple

This pleasing stained-glass project is perfect for your teacher's favorite morning brew, or as a desktop pencil holder!

Callie's Dress

Design by Ann Butler

Materials

- Child's size turtleneck sweater
- 1 yard fabric of choice
- Matching sewing thread
- 12" square HeatnBond Lite fusible adhesive from Therm O Web
- Glittering gold dimensional paint from Tulip
- Pinking shears
- Sewing machine
- Hand-sewing needle
- T-shirt painting board or cardboard

Be sure to choose a fabric with pretty designs that can be cut out and fused to the turtleneck top for this colorful outfit!

Project Notes

Refer to photo throughout.

Refer to manufacturer's instructions for using iron-on adhesive.

Sample was made using a child's size large (10–12) turtleneck.

Instructions

1. Wash turtleneck and fabric without using fabric softener; dry and press as needed.

2. Cut off turtleneck 3" below child's waist.

3. *Skirt:* Cut two 13" x 45" strips from fabric;

stitch a narrow hem along one long side of each piece (this will be dress hem). Lay fabric pieces together right sides facing; sew along 13" edges using ⅜" seam allowance. Sew gathering stitch along top raw edge of skirt. To make gathers easily, pull out about 2 feet of thread from needle on sewing machine, then set machine for widest zigzag stitch and longest seam length. Zigzag over the pulled-out thread for "instant" gathers.

4. With right sides facing,

pin bottom edge of turtleneck to gathered edge of skirt, adjusting gathers evenly. Sew together using ½" seam allowance.

5. Fuse adhesive to wrong side of remaining fabric. Cut desired shapes from fused fabric; arrange on turtleneck and fuse in place.

6. Place top of dress over T-shirt painting board or cardboard to hold it smooth and flat. Outline fabric shapes with gold dimensional paint and add other painted decorations as desired. Let dry.

7. *Bow:* From fused fabric, cut two 6" x 4½" rectangles; peel off backing and place pieces together, fused sides facing. Fuse. Using pinking shears, cut fused fabric into 5½" x 3" piece for bow and ½" x 2" strip for center band. Fan-fold bow; place band around center and stitch tightly. Position bow at waistline of dress left of center; sew in place. ❀

Apples for Teacher continued from page 114

Leaves

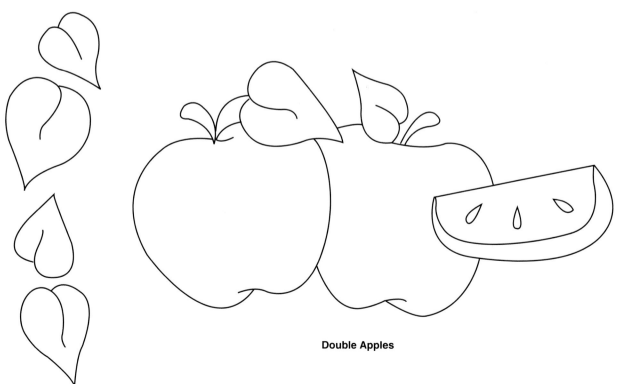

Double Apples

ials of wedding bubbles are available at party supply stores. Pick up a bunch and turn them into wonderful party favors in personalized colors.

Beaded Bubble Necklace

Design by Barbara Woolley

Materials

Each Necklace

- Plastic vial of wedding bubbles
- 1 yard ⅛"-wide satin ribbon in desired color
- Small piece of thin fabric
- Clear glass beads without holes from Craftware
- Red Line double-sided adhesive tape sheets from Craftware
- White tacky craft glue
- Old plate or paper plate

Project Note

Refer to photo throughout.

Instructions

1. Glue fabric to bottle to cover it neatly and smoothly. Do not glue fabric onto area where cap is screwed on, but do cover edge of cap with a strand of ribbon, and cut circles of fabric to cover top of cap and bottom of bottle. Glue ends of ribbon down opposite sides of bottom so bottle hangs from a long loop of ribbon.

2. Cut a piece of adhesive sheet to fit around bottle; remove backing from one side and apply adhesive around bottle.

3. Spread beads on plate in a solid single layer. Peel remaining paper from adhesive on bottle and lay sticky side down in beads, turning bottle to cover adhesive surface completely. Repeat steps 2 and 3 to cover remaining sections of bottle and cap. Let beaded bottle sit undisturbed for 24 hours to allow adhesive to set. ✾

Little fabric scraps make a big impression when they're combined to construct this eye-catching miniature tote bag.

Project Notes

Refer to photo throughout.

Sample project was made with 11 complementary fabrics, including two prints, some solids and tiny prints, plus solid black for the lining and back, and black binding.

Instructions

1. Cut 10 (4" x 1") strips from assorted fabrics. Arrange strips side by side to create a panel of striped fabric; sew together by hand or machine. Lay assembled fabric so stripes run horizontally.

2. Cut a 1¼" x 4" strip from another complementary fabric and sew to the top of the fabric panel; press.

3. Lay lining fabric right side down on work surface. Top with batting, then pieced panel right side up; pin layers in place. Quilt across panel, using a running stitch and stitching on either side of each seam.

4. Cut 4" x 5" piece from backing fabric. With wrong sides facing, sew together using ¼" seam; turn wrong sides out and sew again, catching ¼" seam inside a ½" seam. Turn right side out; press. Sew binding around top edge of tote to finish raw edges.

5. *Strap:* Cut 1 yard binding; sew ends inside tote. Tie knot in binding strap to create the desired length. ✿

Quilted Mini Tote

Design by Samantha McNesby

Materials

- Assorted small fabric scraps in complementary solid colors, patterns and/or prints
- "Fat quarter" (18" x 22½") fabric for backing and lining
- ¼" binding to match or coordinate with fabrics
- Coordinating sewing thread and hand-sewing needle
- Batting at least 4" x 6"
- Sewing machine (optional)

Project Notes

Refer to photo and pattern throughout.

Let paints, ink and sealer dry between applications.

Refer to directions for transferring pattern under "Using Transfer and Graphite Paper" in General Instructions on page 190.

Refer to directions for dry-brushing under "Painting Techniques" in General Instructions on page 191.

Instructions

1. Apply glue to one long edge of each slat; place slats facedown, side by side, and press glued edges together, wiping off excess glue. Apply glue to one side of each craft stick and lay across slats to glue them into one 7³⁄₁₆" x 5⅝" panel. Let glue dry.

2. Turn wooden panel right side up. Transfer window pattern to panel; paint window baby blue. Paint remainder of panel primary yellow on all surfaces.

3. Dry-brush a few light strokes of titanium white across center of window to represent reflection highlights. Using black marker, outline yellow panel and window.

4. *Children:* Glue round head plugs (noses) to centers of 1¼" circles (heads); paint faces flesh tone. Using cotton-tip swab, dab on cheeks of boysenberry pink; using tip of brush handle, dot on eyes with lamp black; using toothpick dipped in

School Bus Salute

Design by Reba Campbell

Materials

- Wooden products from Forster: 2 (7³⁄₁₆" x 2¹³⁄₁₆") slats, 3 craft sticks, 1 jumbo craft stick, 3 (1¼") Woodsies circles, 2 (¾") Woodsies circles, 4 (⅜") Woodsies circles, 2 (1" x ½") rectangles, 3 (³⁄₁₆") round head button plugs

- Americana acrylic paints from DecoArt: titanium white #DA1, boysenberry pink #DA29, baby blue #DA42, lamp black #DA67, slate grey #DA68, flesh tone #DA78, Santa red #DA170, primary yellow #DA201

- ½" paintbrush
- Transfer paper
- Cotton-tip swab
- Toothpick
- ZIG Millennium markers from EK Success Ltd.: 03 pure black, 01 rust
- Thick craft glue
- Masking tape
- Clear matte sealer
- Yarn or doll hair
- Craft drill with small bit
- Fine wire or other hanger

Delight that special school bus driver with a cheerful gift sporting a trio of smiling faces.

titanium white, add three tiny highlight dots near top of each cheek and add highlight dot to each eye.

5. Using black marker, draw smiles and eyebrows; outline each cheek with tiny dots. Using rust marker, add freckles to one nose. Glue heads in window.

6. Paint jumbo craft stick (bumper) slate grey; outline with black marker and add tiny highlight dots of lamp black paint.

7. Paint remaining circles and rectangles Santa red; add highlight dots with toothpick dipped in titanium white.

8. Glue ¾" red circles in upper corners; glue rectangles below window near sides; glue bumper near bottom; glue two ⅜" circles at each end of bumper for lights.

9. Paint "SCHOOL BUS" with lamp black paint; add "Number One" and "Driver" with black marker. Personalize bumper as desired.

10. Spray panel with sealer; let dry.

11. Cut yarn or doll hair in various lengths; tie around center with another piece. Glue one cluster of hair at top of each face.

12. Drill holes in top of panel; add wire hanger, inserting wire from back to front and curling ends to secure. ❀

School Bus Salute

Birthday Candles Duo

Designs by Paula Bales

Materials

Each Project

- Household sponge
- Apple Barrel acrylic paints from Plaid: spring green, yellow, berry red, true blue, white, purple
- Paintbrushes: #2 shader, #3/0 detail round
- Stylus or pin with round head

Gift Sack

- 5¼" x 8½" white paper sack
- ZIG Memory System 05 black Millennium marker

T-Shirt

- Child's white T-shirt
- Water-soluble marker
- Licorice Apple Barrel acrylic paint from Plaid
- ZIG Memory System 08 black Millennium marker
- T-shirt painting board
- Iron
- Waxed paper

Project Note

Refer to photo and patterns throughout.

Gift Sack

1. Dampen sponge; squeeze out excess water. Referring to pattern for T-shirt, draw separate patterns for five candles and a single flame on sponge using marker; cut out.

2. Applying a different color of paint to each candle sponge, sponge one spring green candle, one purple, one yellow, one berry red and one true blue candle onto front of sack.

3. Paint white diagonal stripes down each candle. Using stylus dipped in paint, decorate candles with dots: spring green dots on berry red candle, purple dots on spring green candle, yellow dots on purple candle, true blue dots on yellow candle and berry red dots on true blue candle.

4. Apply yellow paint to candle flame sponge and stamp a flame above each candle. Add a white highlight line.

5. Paint yellow dashes around candles over surface of sack.

6. Using black marker, outline candles and add details.

"Happy Birthday to Me!" T-Shirt

1. Place T-shirt painting board inside T-shirt. Slide T-shirt pattern between T-shirt painting board and T-shirt; outline pattern on shirt with water-soluble marker.

2. Repeat steps 1–4 as for Gift Sack, stamping candles onto T-shirt as pattern shows.

3. Using #2 shader, paint lettering with licorice paint and add candle wicks; use the end of the brush to paint black dots.

4. Paint yellow dashes around design over surface of shirt.

5. Outline candles and flames and add other details with black marker.

6. Heat iron to hot setting, no steam. Place waxed paper over painted area and iron over design for approximately two minutes to heat-set painting. ✿

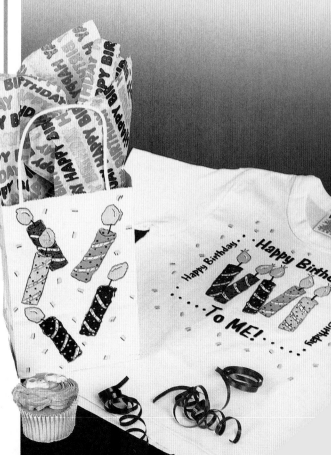

Simple stamped candles are the stars of this pleasing pair—a versatile gift sack and a "Happy Birthday to Me!" T-shirt.

Happy Birthday

Happy Birthday

TO ME!

"Happy Birthday To Me" T-Shirt

Happy Birthday

Foam Fridgie Magnets

Designs by Bev Shenefield

Materials

Each Magnet
- Mini spring clothespin from Forster
- White craft glue
- 1" adhesive-back magnet strip

First Place
- Blue Fun Foam from Westrim
- Gold glitter dimensional paint
- Decorative paper edgers

Artist's Palette
- Tan Fun Foam from Westrim
- Ceramcoat acrylic paints from Delta Technical Coatings Inc.: bright yellow #2027, Copen blue #2051, hunter green #2471, bright red #2503
- Scruffy paintbrush
- Black medium-point permanent marking pen

Grade A Kid
- White Fun Foam from Westrim
- Black fine-point permanent marking pen

Project Note
Refer to photo and patterns throughout.

First Place
1. Using scissors, cut two strips 1" x 4" from blue craft foam. Fold in half lengthwise; cut diagonally from fold to corner, starting ½" up from bottom.

2. Cut circle of rosette from blue craft foam using paper edgers.

3. Add simulated outline stitch inside circle with gold glitter paint. Let dry. Print "1st PLACE" inside inner circle.

4. Glue strips together at slight angle along top edge; glue tops of strips to wrong side of circle. Glue one side of clothespin on top of strips on back; glue magnet strip to other side of clothespin above spring. Let dry.

Artist's Palette
1. Cut palette from tan craft foam.

2. Using scruffy brush, dab puddles of paint thickly on palette; let dry.

3. Using marking pen, print "IN HOUSE ARTIST" on palette.

 se these fun foam magnets to display your masterpieces in the family art gallery (a.k.a. refrigerator)!

4. Glue one side of clothespin to back of palette; glue magnet strip to other side of clothespin above spring. Let dry.

Grade A Kid

1. Cut milk bottle from white craft foam.

2. Using marking pen, print "GRADE A KID" on bottle and add detail lines to represent lip of milk bottle.

3. Glue one side of clothespin to back of palette; glue magnet strip to other side of clothespin above spring. Let dry. ❀

Grade A Kid
Cut 1 from white

Artist's Palette
Cut 1 from tan

First Place
Cut 1 from blue

Fanciful Felt Bookmarks

Designs by Nancy Marshall

Materials

- Small amounts of Rainbow Felt Classic from Kunin: harvest gold #J55, pink punch #0G9, baby pink #053, red #064, yellow #351, apple green #458, white #550, baby blue #660, royal blue #678, silver gray #928, black #937
- 12"–18" piece ⅜"-wide satin or grosgrain ribbon: green, royal blue, pink
- Light fabric marker or tailor's chalk
- ¼" round hole punch
- Tacky craft glue

Project Notes

Refer to photo and patterns throughout.

Use 12" ribbon for paperbacks, and 18" ribbon for larger hardcover books.

Romantic Hearts

1. Cut two small hearts and two large hearts from pink punch; cut two sets of leaves, reversing one, from apple green. Using hole punch, punch eight baby pink circles.

2. Lay apple green leaf set on each large heart; glue in place. Arrange four baby pink circles on stem for flowers; glue in place.

3. Sandwich one end of pink ribbon between large hearts and other end between small hearts; glue.

Rocket Ship

1. Cut one rocket body from silver gray; cut two rocket fins, reversing one, two stripes and two boosters from red; cut two stars from yellow. Cut also one ⁷⁄₁₆"-diameter circle from baby blue.

2. Without gluing pieces together, arrange rocket body, fins and boosters atop royal blue felt; trace around shapes ⅛" from edges with light fabric marker or tailor's chalk. Cut out royal blue shape.

3. Sandwich one end of royal blue ribbon between yellow stars; glue. Sandwich other end between royal blue background and silver gray rocket body; glue in place. Glue on red rocket fins, boosters and stripes and baby blue porthole.

Garden Bookmark

1. Cut two sunflowers and four bee stripes from yellow felt, one pair bee wings from white, and two bee bodies from black. Cut also two ¾"-diameter circles from harvest gold.

2. Glue two stripes to each bee body; glue body to each set of white wings. Sandwich one end of green ribbon between bee halves and glue in place.

3. Glue harvest gold circle to center of each yellow sunflower; sandwich other end of ribbon between sunflowers and glue in place. ❈

S

atin ribbons are sandwiched between colorful felt shapes to make these delightful bookmarks!

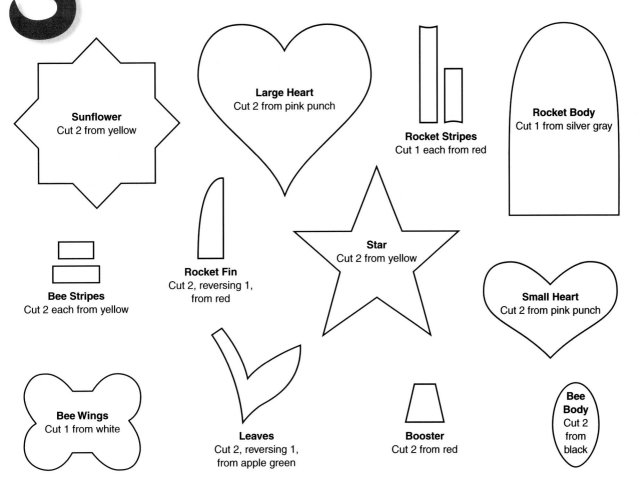

Sunflower
Cut 2 from yellow

Large Heart
Cut 2 from pink punch

Rocket Stripes
Cut 1 each from red

Rocket Body
Cut 1 from silver gray

Bee Stripes
Cut 2 each from yellow

Rocket Fin
Cut 2, reversing 1, from red

Star
Cut 2 from yellow

Small Heart
Cut 2 from pink punch

Bee Wings
Cut 1 from white

Leaves
Cut 2, reversing 1, from apple green

Booster
Cut 2 from red

Bee Body
Cut 2 from black

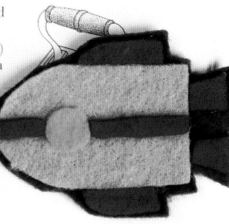

Fun Felt Pillows

Designs by Deborah Spofford

Materials

Daisy Pillow

- Kunin Felt: 5" x 4½" piece each bright green, white, yellow, royal blue and violet; 2" x 3" orange; 2 (16") squares fuchsia
- 9 daisy buttons in assorted colors by James Button & Trim
- Cotton embroidery floss: yellow, bright green, royal blue, orange, white, violet
- Fuchsia sewing thread

Geometrics Pillow

- Kunin Felt: 4½" square each fuchsia, orange, yellow, royal blue and violet; 2 (15" x 19¼") rectangles bright green
- 4 buttons in assorted complementary bright colors
- Cotton embroidery floss: yellow, bright green, royal blue, orange, pink, violet
- Bright green sewing thread

Each Pillow

- 12" square pillow form
- ⅛ yard HeatnBond Lite iron-on adhesive from Therm O Web
- Pressing paper
- Iron
- Embroidery needle
- Sewing machine

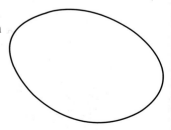

Project Notes

Refer to photo and patterns throughout. Follow manufacturer's instructions for using iron-on adhesive.

Daisy Pillow

1. Fuse iron-on adhesive to back of all small felt pieces.

2. Cut one daisy each from bright green, white, yellow, royal blue and violet felt; do not cut out centers from daisies. Cut one separate oval center each from bright green, yellow, royal blue, orange and violet felt.

3. Peel paper backing from daisies; arrange on one of fuchsia felt squares. Cover felt with pressing paper and fuse daisies to pillow front with iron. Peel backing from centers; place centers on daisies: royal blue center on yellow daisy, orange on royal blue, yellow on bright green, violet on white and bright green on violet. Cover with pressing paper and fuse in place.

4. Using matching colors of embroidery floss, blanket-stitch around each daisy and daisy center.

5. Sew a daisy button to center of each felt daisy; sew remaining buttons between daisies.

6. Place fuchsia pillow front and back together, wrong sides facing. Using sewing machine and fuchsia thread, stitch around pillow, using 1½" seam allowance and leaving an opening for pillow form. Stuff pillow with form and stitch opening closed.

Geometrics Pillow

1. Fuse iron-on adhesive to back of all 4½" felt squares.

2. Cut daisy from fuchsia felt square, triangle from orange, starburst from yellow, crisscross from violet and ring from royal blue. Cut out centers from each felt piece.

3. Peel paper backing from shapes; arrange within a 10½"-square area in center of one of the bright green felt rectangles; on sample, crisscross is placed in center and remaining shapes are placed in corners of design area. Cover felt with pressing paper and fuse shapes to pillow front with iron.

4. Using contrasting colors of embroidery floss, blanket-stitch around each shape and center. On sample, orange triangle was stitched with royal blue floss, starburst with orange, ring with pink, crisscross with bright green, and daisy with yellow.

5. Sew buttons between felt shapes using assorted contrasting colors of floss.

6. Place bright green pillow front and back together, right sides facing. Using sewing machine and bright green thread, stitch along long sides of pillow using ¾" seam allowance. Turn pillow right side out. Machine-stitch along one short end 2½" from edge. Insert pillow form; pin open end closed 2½" from edge and machine-stitch closed.

7. Using violet embroidery floss on one end and orange floss on the other, blanket-stitch around open edges of pillow. ❀

Patterns continued on page 131

Daisy Center
For Daisy Pillow, cut 1 each from royal blue, orange, yellow, bright green and violet felt

K ids will have a ball and exercise their creativity by cutting colorful felt shapes to make these simple flower power pillows.

"Whitewashed" Wooden Frames

Designs by Samantha McNesby

Materials

Each Frame

- 6" x 5" wooden frame
- Wooden folk-art stars: 2 (1½"), 1 (1")
- Paintbrushes: flat brush and old, scruffy paintbrush
- Craft glue or hot-glue gun
- Photo
- Masking tape (optional)
- Sawtooth hanger

"Dream"

- 1" wooden letters to spell "DREAM"
- Americana acrylic paints from DecoArt: white wash #DA2, desert turquoise #DA44

"Imagine"

- 1" wooden letters to spell "IMAGINE"
- Americana acrylic paints from DecoArt: white wash #DA2, deep periwinkle #DA212

Capture those once-in-a-lifetime moments on film—and then preserve them forever in these dreamy frames.

Project Notes

Refer to photo throughout. There is no need to sand the wooden pieces; their rough edges enhance the "weathered" effect.

Refer to directions for dry-brushing under "Painting Techniques" in General Instructions on page 191.

Let all paints dry between applications.

"Dream" Frame

1. Paint front and edges of frame, stars and letters with desert turquoise.

2. Using scruffy brush, dry-brush frame, letters and stars with white wash, whisking brush over surface until the desired appearance is achieved.

3. Glue letters across top of frame and stars across bottom. Let glue cure for 24 hours before gluing or taping photo in place on back of frame. Attach sawtooth hanger or other hanger to back of frame.

"Imagine" Frame

Follow instructions for "Dream" Frame, substituting deep periwinkle paint for desert turquoise and "IMAGINE" letters. ❧

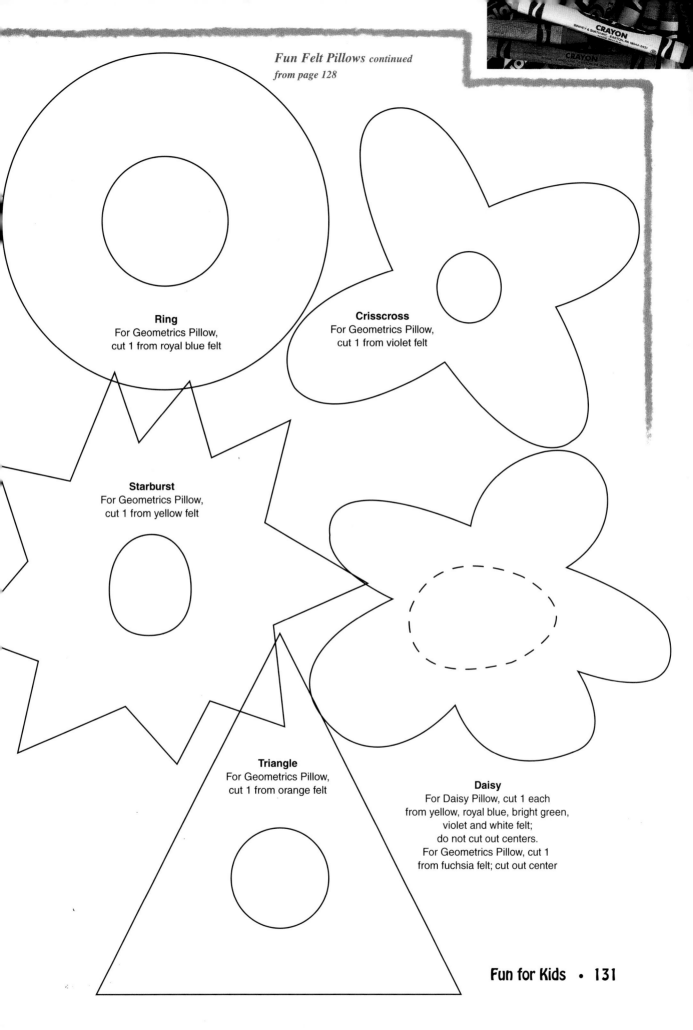

Ring
For Geometrics Pillow,
cut 1 from royal blue felt

Crisscross
For Geometrics Pillow,
cut 1 from violet felt

Starburst
For Geometrics Pillow,
cut 1 from yellow felt

Triangle
For Geometrics Pillow,
cut 1 from orange felt

Daisy
For Daisy Pillow, cut 1 each
from yellow, royal blue, bright green,
violet and white felt;
do not cut out centers.
For Geometrics Pillow, cut 1
from fuchsia felt; cut out center

Summer Bugs & Blooms Jumbo Can

Design by Laura Scott

Materials

- Fun Foam craft foam from Westrim: 1 sheet lime green #15, 1 sheet light blue #20, small amounts black #2, white #5, red #8, purple #12, pink #13, yellow #25, rose #32, orange #34
- 18-ounce breakfast-drink can
- Hold-the-Foam craft-foam glue from Beacon Adhesives
- Glue brush
- ZIG black twin-tip permanent marker from EK Success Ltd.
- ¼" round hole punch
- Rubber bands
- Small scissors with fine pointed tips

 **large recycled can becomes a colorful container for markers and other art supplies.**

Project Note

Refer to photo and patterns throughout.

Instructions

1. Cut light blue craft foam to fit around can. Apply a liberal amount of glue to outside of can; place foam on can, overlapping edges slightly. Wrap can with rubber bands until glue is dry.

2. *Grass:* Cut 1⅝"-wide strip of lime green foam to fit around can; trim one long edge in a wavy pattern. Cut 1"–1¼" vertical strips in varying widths along wavy edge leaving ¼" uncut along straight edge. Glue straight edge along bottom of can over light blue foam.

3. *Flowers:* Cut 12 petals each from pink and orange; cut six petals from rose; cut two large stems, three small stems, seven large leaves and three small leaves from lime green; cut five centers from yellow.

4. *Bumblebees:* Cut two bee bodies from black, three stripes for each bee from yellow and two wings from white. Glue stripes to bodies; glue pointed end of one wing over stripes on each bumblebee. Set aside.

5. *Butterflies:* Cut two butterfly wings each from rose and pink and two butterfly bodies from black. Using hole punch, punch

12 dots from purple; set aside.

6. *Ladybug:* Cut one ladybug body from red and one head from black; set aside.

7. Using bullet tip of black marker, write "summer bugs and summer blooms" in small letters along top part of can in a wavy line; draw a dashed line around lettering with loops here and there.

8. Glue flower stems behind grass, positioning them around can ¾"–1" above bottom edge and alternating large and small stems. Glue six petals around the top of each stem with tips of petals touching each other. Glue

leaves to stems as desired, and glue a yellow center over the tips of petals and top of stem on each flower.

9. Glue bumblebees near top edge of can. Glue butterfly bodies in place below lettering and between flowers; glue wings to each side of body. Glue three purple dots onto each wing.

10. Using fine tip of black marker throughout, add details shown on patterns and add antennae to ladybug and butterflies; add four small dots to each butterfly wing dot. Use bullet tip to mark black dots on ladybug's body. ✿

Small Leaf
Cut 3 from lime green

Flower Center
Cut 5 from yellow

Butterfly Wing
Cut 2 from rose
and 2 from pink

Ladybug Body
Cut 1 from red

Butterfly Body
Cut 2 from black

Bee Wing
Cut 2 from white

Large Stem
Cut 2 from lime green

Small Stem
Cut 3 from lime green

Petal
Cut 6 from rose and
12 each from pink and orange

Ladybug Head
Cut 1 from black

Large Leaf
Cut 7 from lime green

Bee Body & Stripes
Cut 2 bodies from black;
cut stripes from yellow

Happy Holidays

From Valentine's Day through Thanksgiving, celebrating the holidays has never been as much fun as it is now! Fun and festive gifts and decorations are just what you need to add a sparkling, handcrafted touch to the holidays!

Cupid's Arrow Door Hanger

Design by Mary Cardoni

Decorate your door or dress up your bulletin board with this cute valentine design.

Materials
- Cardboard
- Craft batting
- Red felt
- Gold fabric or vinyl
- Craft glue
- Sewing needle and red thread
- Gold paper candy cup
- 2"-wide clear tape
- Gold paper heart-shaped doily
- Gold cord

Project Note
Refer to patterns and photo throughout.

Instructions
1. Cut small heart and large heart shapes from cardboard, batting and felt. Cut large and small heart covers from red felt.

2. Glue batting hearts to corresponding cardboard hearts. With sewing needle and thread, sew running stitch around edge of each heart cover. Fit over batting-covered heart and gently pull thread to snug fabric into place. Sew back and forth over back of heart to hold felt firmly. Glue small and large felt heart shapes onto wrong sides of covered hearts for backing.

3. Cut arrow shaft and point from cardboard; cut arrow shaft cover, point covering and point backing from gold fabric or vinyl.

4. Glue gold arrow shaft covering around cardboard arrow shaft. Glue arrow shaft to top of arrow point. Cover point with gold fabric, turning under lower tabs and wrapping side tabs to back as shown. Glue point backing in place on back of arrow.

5. Sew arrow in place on front of large heart. Glue small heart over arrow.

6. To make "feathers" for arrow, flatten gold paper candy cup; cut into 10 equal wedges. Referring to Fig. 1, press wedges into rows on sticky side of 2" tape. Cover with another piece of tape so gold paper is enclosed. Trim excess tape from sides.

7. Using tape-covered gold piece as a template, cut a matching piece from gold fabric; glue fabric to back of tape-covered feathers. Run bead of glue down center of feathers; glue to wrong side of arrow shaft at end.

8. Cut small gold heart for front from center of gold paper heart-shaped doily; glue to center front of design.

9. Sew gold cord hanging loop to back of heart. ✿

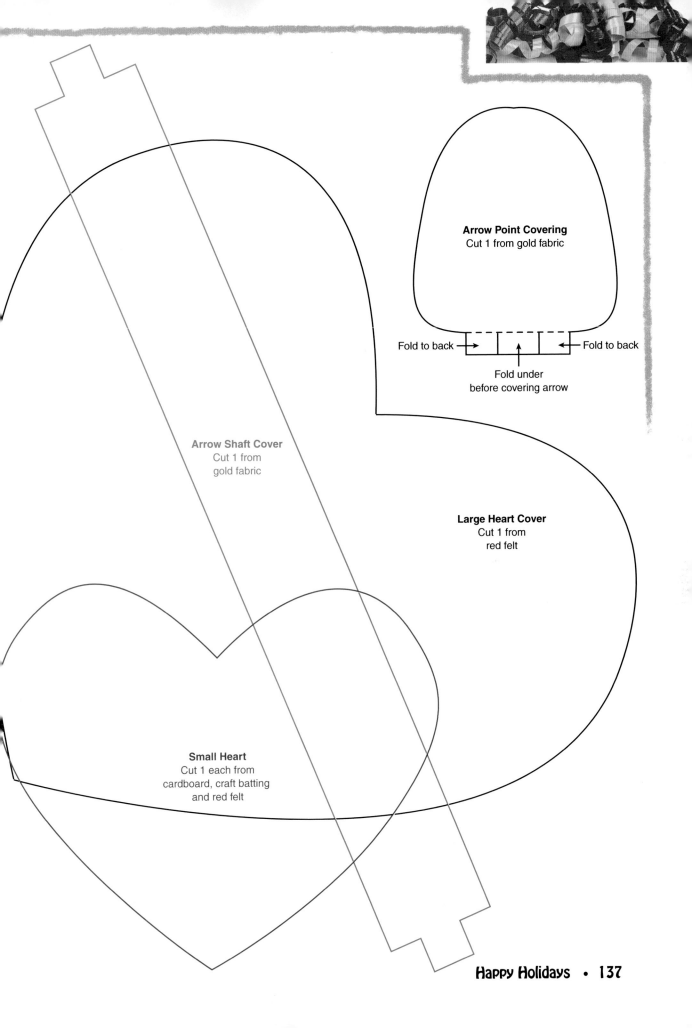

Arrow Point Covering
Cut 1 from gold fabric

Fold to back →   ← Fold to back

Fold under
before covering arrow

Arrow Shaft Cover
Cut 1 from
gold fabric

Large Heart Cover
Cut 1 from
red felt

Small Heart
Cut 1 each from
cardboard, craft batting
and red felt

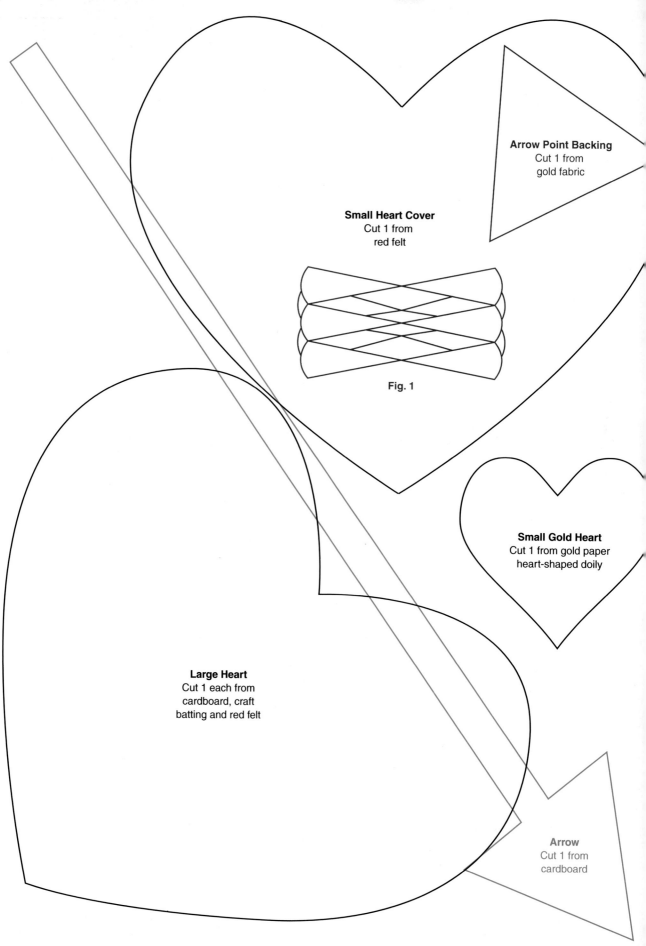

Arrow Point Backing
Cut 1 from
gold fabric

Small Heart Cover
Cut 1 from
red felt

Fig. 1

Small Gold Heart
Cut 1 from gold paper
heart-shaped doily

Large Heart
Cut 1 each from
cardboard, craft
batting and red felt

Arrow
Cut 1 from
cardboard

Nothing says "I love you!" like a handmade valentine. You'll find it easy to turn out many of these charming cards decorated with fun fabrics!

Project Notes
Refer to photo throughout.

Follow manufacturer's instructions for fusing fusible web.

Instructions
1. Glue strip of lace along each side edge of card from front to back.

2. Adhere fusible web to wrong sides of fabrics. Cut four hearts in graduating sizes from fused fabrics.

3. Position hearts on front of card; fuse hearts in place. Let cool.

4. Write "Be Mine" or other message on front of card with red calligraphy pen. Add a border of dots around the hearts. ❀

Be Mine

Design by Blanche Lind

Materials
- 5" x 7" white card stock
- 20" piece white ⅞"-wide lace with red hearts
- Craft glue
- Fusible web
- Fabric scraps in 4 red-and-white prints
- Red calligraphy pen
- Iron

Fun 'n' Fuzzy Baskets

Designs by Kathy Wegner

Materials

Each Basket

- Clean, empty 6-ounce tuna can
- Woodsies wooden shapes from Forster: 4 small circles, 2 large circles, 4 medium teardrops
- Aleene's Premium-Coat acrylic paint: white #OC 173
- Fiesta pink #65303 matte 3-D paint from Tulip
- Fine-point black permanent marker
- Craft adhesive
- Paintbrushes: small flat, old scruffy brush
- Toothpick

Easter Eggs

- 2" x 10" strip groovy green Shaggy Plush felt from Kunin
- Woodsies wooden shapes from Forster: 4 large eggs
- Lime Stretch-A-Roo curled chenille stem from Fibre-Craft
- Aleene's Premium-Coat acrylic paints: true yellow #OC 127, true blue #OC 151, true violet #OC 163, true fuchsia #OC 169

Crunchy Carrots

- 2" x 10" strip purple passion Shaggy Plush felt from Kunin
- Woodsies wooden shapes from Forster: 4 additional medium teardrops, 4 small triangles
- Purple Stretch-A-Roo curled chenille stem from Fibre-Craft
- Additional Aleene's Premium-Coat acrylic paints: true orange #OC 115, medium lime #OC 132

Project Notes

Refer to photo throughout.

Refer to directions for base-coating and dry-brushing under "Painting Techniques" in General Instructions on page 191.

Let all paints and ink dry between applications.

Easter Eggs

1. Base-coat all wooden pieces with two coats white acrylic paint, painting all surfaces of four

medium teardrops, and front and edges of all remaining pieces.

2. *Bunnies:* Using white throughout, paint four medium teardrops (ears), two large circles (heads) and four small circles (cheeks). Using old scruffy brush, dry-brush fiesta pink very lightly down centers of ears and on cheek areas of heads. Glue rounded ends of ears behind each head; glue two cheeks to each head so that edges touch in center. Using toothpick and fiesta pink, paint small triangular nose between cheeks. Using fine-point marker, add eyes, dot freckles on cheeks, and add small line details at base of ears.

3. *Easter eggs:* Paint one egg each true yellow, true violet, true fuchsia and true blue. Add decorations as desired with fine-point black marker and paints.

4. *Basket:* Glue felt strip around can leaving excess at top. Fold excess felt down into inside of can and glue. Leave chenille stem intact without stretching. Glue ends inside can for handle.

5. *Finishing:* Glue bunnies onto felt on basket opposite each other, one on center front and one at center back. Glue two

Continued on page 144

Turn empty tuna cans into the stars of your holiday table! Fuzzy felt in groovy colors does the trick!

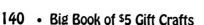

ead over heels in his haste to treat you to some special eggs, this Easter bunny also brings a touch of springtime whimsy!

Bouncing Bunny Ornament

Design by Marilyn Gossett

Materials

- Wooden products from Lara's Crafts: 1¼" x 1" oval, 2" heart, 1" heart, 4 (1¼") stockings, ½" button plug, 3 (⅝" x ⅞") split eggs
- ½" ribbon roses: 1 blue, 2 pink
- Green and ivory tiny-check fabric: ¼" x 8" strip; 5 (⅜") squares
- Wood glue and tacky craft glue
- Ceramcoat acrylic paints from Delta: ivory #2036, blue heaven #2037, spice tan #2063, GP purple #2091, custard #2448, white #2505, black #2506, pink parfait #2525
- Ceramcoat satin varnish from Delta
- Paintbrushes: #12 shader, ¼" angle shader, #0 liner
- Toothpick or stylus
- Black extra-fine-tip marker
- 16" piece 24-gauge brass wire
- Wire cutters
- Needle-nose pliers
- Craft drill with small bit

Project Notes

Refer to photo and pattern throughout.

See directions for floating under "Painting Techniques" in General Instructions on page 191.

Let all paints, ink and varnish dry between applications.

Assembly

1. Drill holes in stocking shapes for paws (use a needle, wire or toothpick to keep holes open as you paint and seal bunny).

2. Glue pieces together: stockings for paws (upper ones pointing out, bottom ones pointing in), then large heart for body, small heart for ears, oval for head and button plug for tail. Let glue dry thoroughly.

Painting

1. Paint bunny ivory. Paint sweater on body and bottom paws pink parfait; add custard dots, dipping tip

Continued on page 144

Easter Egg Mates

Designs by Marilyn Gossett

Materials

Each Egg Mate

- 3" hinged plastic Easter egg: yellow for chick and duck, lavender for bunny
- 1¾"–2" ⅛"-thick scalloped wooden heart cutout
- Sandpaper
- Craft foam: orange for chick and duck, purple for bunny
- 2 (9mm) round black wiggly eyes
- ⅝" circle cut from compressed sponge
- Ceramcoat acrylic paints from Delta: white #2505, pink parfait pink #2525
- #12 shader paintbrush
- Hot-glue gun
- Shredded crinkled paper: green for chick, pink for bunny, lavender for duck
- Candies

Chick

- 2 yellow feathers
- 2" straw hat
- 1" silk daisy
- Natural raffia
- Scrap of green sheet moss
- Opaque yellow #2509 Ceramcoat acrylic paint from Delta

Bunny

- 8" purple curling ribbon
- 2" straw hat
- 1" purple silk rose
- Natural raffia
- Scrap of green sheet moss
- Eggplant #2486 Ceramcoat acrylic paint from Delta
- Black permanent marking pen

Duck

- 8" ¼"-wide purple satin ribbon
- 1 yellow feather
- Pumpkin #2042 Ceramcoat acrylic paint from Delta

Bunny Nose
Cut 1 from purple
craft foam

Chick Beak
Cut 1 from orange
craft foam

Bunny Ears
Cut 1 from purple
craft foam

Duck Bill
Cut 1 from
orange craft foam

Project Notes

Refer to photo and patterns throughout.

Let all paints and ink dry between applications.

Chick

1. *Feet:* Paint heart cutout opaque yellow on all surfaces.

2. Sand base (broad end) of egg; glue to painted heart with point of heart facing back and egg's hinge in center back.

3. *Cheeks:* Expand sponge circle in water to make a "stamp"; press out water. Dip sponge into pink parfait paint; blot off most of paint onto paper towel. "Stamp" top half of egg once for each cheek. Highlight cheeks with a tiny white dot applied with tip of paintbrush handle.

4. Cut beak from orange craft foam. Fold in half along dashed line; glue fold to top half of egg between cheeks. Glue on eyes.

5. *Wings:* Cut 3" from top of each feather; glue to top half of egg on back so feather tips extend evenly along sides.

6. Embellish hat with daisy, sheet moss and a small bow of natural raffia. Glue hat to head. Glue a small piece of

feather to underside of brim at center front for "hair." Fill egg with paper shreds and candies.

Bunny

1. Repeat steps 1–3 as for Chick, substituting eggplant paint for opaque yellow. Using black marking pen, add three whisker dots to each cheek, and draw ½" vertical line between cheeks.

2. Cut ears and nose from purple craft foam. Glue bottom edge of ears to hat brim in front of crown. Glue nose at top of vertical line on bunny's face; glue on eyes.

3. Embellish hat with sheet moss, ribbon curls, rose and a small bow of natural raffia. Glue hat to head. Fill egg with paper shreds and candies.

Duck

1. Repeat steps 1–4 as for Chick, substituting bill for beak and pumpkin paint for opaque yellow.

2. Cut 1" piece from yellow feather; glue to top of head for "hair."

3. Tie ribbon in a bow; trim ends at an angle. Glue bow to top edge of egg's bottom half at center front. ❀

Fun 'n' Fuzzy Baskets continued from page 140

eggs between bunnies on each side, spacing them evenly. Let glue dry completely before handling basket.

Crunchy Carrots

1. Follow steps 1 and 2 as for Easter Eggs basket.

2. *Carrots:* Paint four medium teardrops true orange for carrots and four small triangles medium lime for carrot tops. Add details to carrots and leaf curls to tops with fine-point black marker.

3. Repeat step 4 as for Easter Eggs basket using purple felt and purple chenille stem.

4. *Finishing:* Glue bunnies onto felt on basket opposite each other, one on center front and one at center back. Glue two carrots and their tops evenly spaced on each side of bunnies, with tops toward bunnies. Let glue dry completely before handling basket. ❀

Bouncing Bunny Ornament continued from page 141

of paintbrush handle in custard paint and touching it to sweater, redipping before each to keep dots uniform in size. Paint tail white.

2. *Face:* Blush cheeks and inner ears with pink parfait. Using stylus dipped in black, dot on eyes. Paint heart-shaped nose pink parfait. Using stylus dipped in white, add highlight dots to eyes, cheeks and ears.

3. Float edges of all wooden pieces with thinned spice tan.

4. Paint one half-egg blue heaven; add GP purple dots with stylus. Paint a second egg custard; add pink parfait wavy lines. Paint last egg GP purple; dot with custard.

5. Seal all pieces with satin varnish.

Finishing

1. *Hanger:* Cut 8" piece of wire; push one end from back to front through hole in one upper paw; twist ring in end to secure on front. Bring wire from back to front through hole in opposite foot; make ring in end of wire to hold it securely.

2. *Garland:* Repeat as for hanger, threading wire through lower paws. Glue blue heaven egg, blue ribbon rose, custard egg, pink rose and GP purple egg to wire by gluing one of the tiny fabric squares to the back of each piece, sandwiching the wire in between.

3. Tie fabric strip into a shoestring bow with ½" loops and tails. Glue to one side of neck; glue remaining ribbon rose to bow. ❀

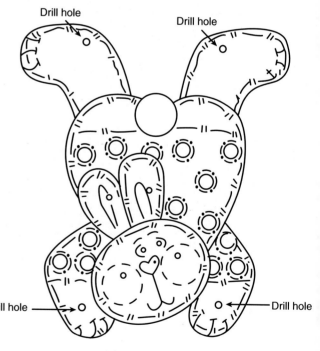

Drill hole   Drill hole

Drill hole   Drill hole

Bouncing Bunny

hip up a batch of these simple, colorful candle lanterns for your holiday celebration—or for any gathering where festive lighting is in order.

Tin-Can Luminarias & Recycled Candles

Designs by Bev Shenefield

Materials

Each Luminaria

- Clean, tall spaghetti-sauce can, labels and 1 end removed
- Goo Gone
- Hammer and nail
- Perm-Enamel products from Delta: surface conditioner and clear gloss glaze
- Rust-resistant spray primer
- Flat white spray paint
- Perm-Enamel paints from Delta: classic navy blue #45016, red red #45033
- Cosmetic sponge
- Marvy fine-line Liquid Gold pen

Each Candle

- Clean 8-ounce tomato-sauce can, 1 end removed
- Discarded candles and/or candle ends
- Candle wicking
- Pencil
- Vegetable oil
- Essential oil (optional)
- Heavy saucepan and large can to fit in it

Project Notes

Refer to photo and patterns throughout.

Let all applications of primer, sealer, paint, ink and glaze dry between applications.

Look for candles—including used and/or broken ones—at yard sales and thrift stores.

They are perfect for making your own candles and are much less expensive than new candles.

Luminarias

1. Remove label glue from spaghetti-sauce can with Goo Gone. Wash and rinse well; let dry. Fill cans with water and reeze 24 hours or until solidly frozen.

2. Place pattern on can with seam in back; tape in place with masking tape if desired. Lay can on heavy towel. With hammer and nail, punch holes around edge of pattern, replacing can in freezer to refreeze as necessary.

3. When can is punched, let ice melt and dry can thoroughly. Wash down can with surface conditioner; let dry. Spray with primer, then with flat white spray paint.

4. Using sponge, paint designs on cans:

"America" hearts— Sponge every other stripe classic navy blue; sponge hearts red red.

"Freedom" stars— Sponge stars classic navy blue; sponge every other stripe red red.

5. Outline motifs and add stripes and lettering with gold pen. Coat cans with clear gloss glaze.

Recycled Candles

1. Coat inside of small can with oil; pour out excess.

2. Tie wick around pencil; lay pencil across top of can and adjust till wick hangs straight to the bottom in center.

3. Place odds and ends of candles in large can; set in pan of hot water and very carefully melt candles over low heat. Add essential oil if desired.

4. Carefully pour melted wax into prepared can to within about ½" of top. Adjust wick as necessary and set aside to harden completely. If wax sinks in the center, add a little more melted wax.

5. When candle is completely hardened, carefully lift it out of the can with the pencil, taking care not to break the wick. If candle resists, run hot water over sides and bottom of can and twist it gently until it releases. Trim wick to about ½" long.

6. Insert candle in luminaria. ❀

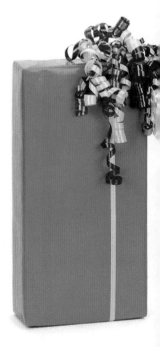

America
Enlarge pattern to 125%

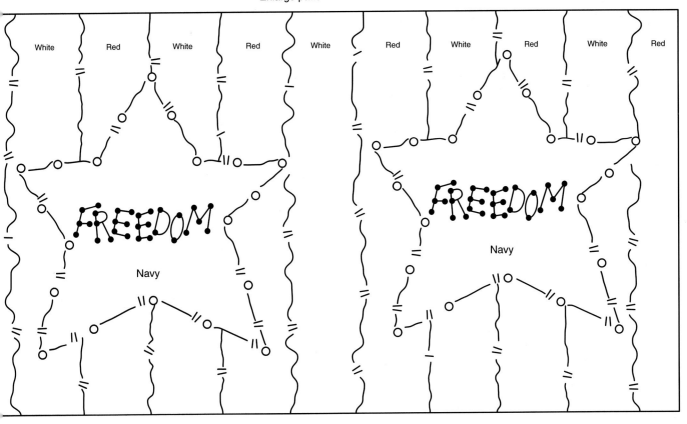

Freedom
Enlarge pattern to 125%

Country Flag Accents

Designs by Kim Lasky

Materials

- Pop-Up Paper products: lamp-shade cover, wastepaper basket, 6" x 7½" and 4" x 5" picture frames, tissue box cover, single and double switch-plate covers, door hanger
- Russet brown Decorator Glaze Paint from Plaid
- Apple Barrel acrylic paints from Plaid: antique white, cardinal crimson, true navy, black
- Paintbrushes: ¾" and #12 flats, #1 script
- Toothbrush

Project Notes

Refer to photo throughout.

Let all paints and glaze dry between applications.

Instructions

1. On paper product, mark off area where true navy field will go; paint area with two coats true navy. Paint remainder of product with two coats antique white.

2. Freehand cardinal crimson stripes the width of the brush across antique white area, using ¾" flat brush for lamp-shade cover and wastepaper basket and #12 flat brush for other products.

3. Randomly paint antique white primitive-style stars of various sizes over navy areas, using two or three coats as needed for complete coverage.

4. Using ¾" flat brush, apply russet brown glaze over entire painted surface, brushing in same direction as stripes.

5. Lightly spatter pieces using toothbrush and a mixture of black paint and a little water. ❀

Spread patriotic pride throughout your entire home with these ingenious home accents. They have the look of antique flags— but they're made of durable heavyweight paper "antiqued" with a brown glaze and spatter-painted "distress" marks.

Foam Leaf Basket

Design by Barbara Matthiessen

Materials

- Basket
- 3 kraft-color paper-covered stem wires
- Craft foam sheets: 1 sheet each orange, yellow and green, and 2" square brown
- ZIG pens from EK Success Ltd.: green and brown pigment writers, and 05 black marking pen
- Craft Foam Glue from Beacon Adhesives
- 2 (1½" x 36") torn fabric strips
- Jute twine
- Stiff paintbrush
- Needle-nose pliers (optional)

Maple Leaf
Cut 2 from orange & 2
from yellow foam

Oak Leaf
Cut 2 from
orange &
2 from
yellow foam

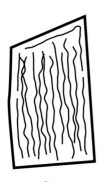

Stem
Cut 1 from brown
foam

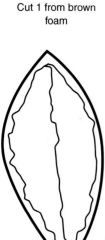

Alder Leaf
Cut 2 from yellow &
4 from green foam

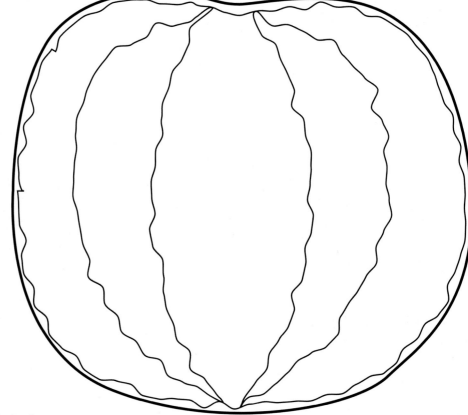

Pumpkin
Cut 1 from orange craft foam

Add a handle to an inexpensive basket and embellish it with foam leaves in fall colors for an attractive autumnal accent piece.

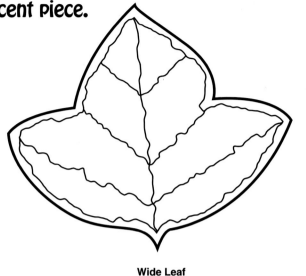

Wide Leaf
Cut 3 from green foam

Project Notes

Refer to photo and patterns throughout.

The number of leaves and pumpkins needed will depend on the size of your basket. Sample basket measures 9" diameter and uses one pumpkin and two oak and two maple leaves cut from orange foam; two maple, two oak and two alder leaves cut from yellow foam; three wide and four alder leaves from green foam; and one pumpkin stem from brown foam.

Instructions

1. Trace leaves as desired onto craft foam using black marking pen. Cut out, turning foam into your scissors and using long, smooth strokes.

2. Using green pen for green leaves and brown pen for all other pieces, shade foam pieces by drawing around the edges and vein lines for a couple of inches, then rubbing over the wet ink with a stiff-bristle paintbrush. When shading edges, brush ink toward the center of the piece.

3. Using black pen, add wiggly outlines and details to all foam pieces.

4. Loosely braid paper-covered stem wires together. Insert ends into sides of basket to form handle base. Using your fingers or needle-nose pliers, bend ends into loops inside basket to hold handle in place.

5. Crisscross fabric strips around stem-wire handle, tying ends in knots at sides of basket.

6. Glue wide green leaf over wire ends inside basket on both sides.

7. *Glue foam leaves to handle:* On sample, two orange maple leaves are glued broad end to broad end at center top; from top down, yellow oak leaf, green alder leaf and yellow alder leaf are glued to handle on each side.

8. *Glue foam pieces to basket front:* On sample, orange pumpkin is glued over yellow maple and orange oak leaves and two green alder leaves; end of brown stem is inserted behind pumpkin at center top; green wide leaf is glued off to one side at top of pumpkin.

9. Tie jute twine in bow around top of handle. ❀

Trick-or-Treat Bag

Design by Kathy Wegner

Materials

- 12" x 10" white paper bag with handles
- Scrapbook papers: 5" x 7" piece each of 2 different black print papers; 5" x 6" piece orange; 2½" x 5" piece candy corn print; 1½" x 2½" piece yellow; 1" square green
- Seagull paper edgers from Fiskars
- Mounting Memories Keepsake glue from Beacon Adhesives
- 2 (12mm) black or glow-in-the-dark wiggly eyes
- Black and orange fine-tip permanent markers

Project Note

Refer to photo and patterns throughout.

Instructions

1. Cut pattern pieces from papers using regular scissors: one pumpkin from orange; one stem from green; one nose and two bat's eyes from yellow. Cut one mound of candy corn from candy-corn print paper. Cut one bat from each of the two black print papers, using paper edgers to cut along bottoms of wings and regular scissors for the rest.

2. Glue candy corn to bag at bottom edge. Glue pumpkin over candy corn; glue stem, nose and wiggly eyes onto pumpkin. Glue bats above pumpkin, overlapping them as shown; glue eyes to bats.

3. Using orange marker, write "Trick or Treat" above bats. Add stars to letters with black marker. Using black marker, draw mouth on pumpkin; add pupils and lines between bats' eyes. ❈

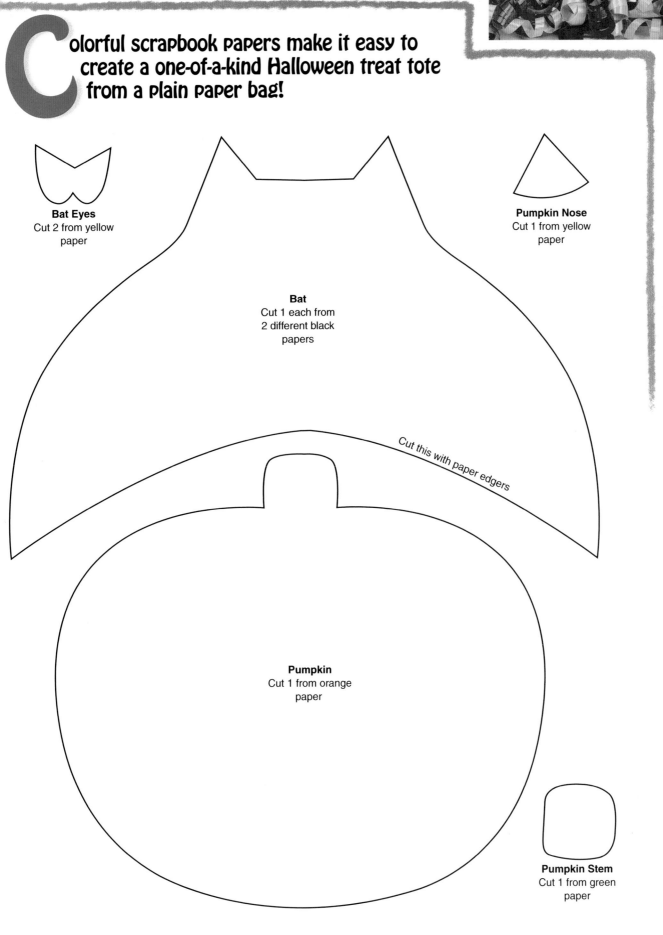

Colorful scrapbook papers make it easy to create a one-of-a-kind Halloween treat tote from a plain paper bag!

Bat Eyes
Cut 2 from yellow
paper

Pumpkin Nose
Cut 1 from yellow
paper

Bat
Cut 1 each from
2 different black
papers

Cut this with paper edgers

Pumpkin
Cut 1 from orange
paper

Pumpkin Stem
Cut 1 from green
paper

Bat Tooth
Cut 2 from white felt

Bat Puppet

Design by Kathy Wegner

Materials

- 10" x 18" piece black Rainbow Plush Felt from Kunin Felt
- Scrap of regular white felt
- Fabric adhesive
- 2 (10mm) black wiggly eyes
- 2" piece white pearl cotton or string

Project Note

Refer to photo and patterns throughout.

Instructions

1. Cut two bats on the fold from black plush felt; cut two teeth from white felt.

2. With wrong sides facing, glue bats together around edges, leaving bottom open.

3. Glue eyes to front of bat. Glue white string in place for smile; glue teeth at smile.

4. Allow glue to dry thoroughly before using. ✹

Place on fold

Bat Puppet
Cut 2 on fold from
black plush felt

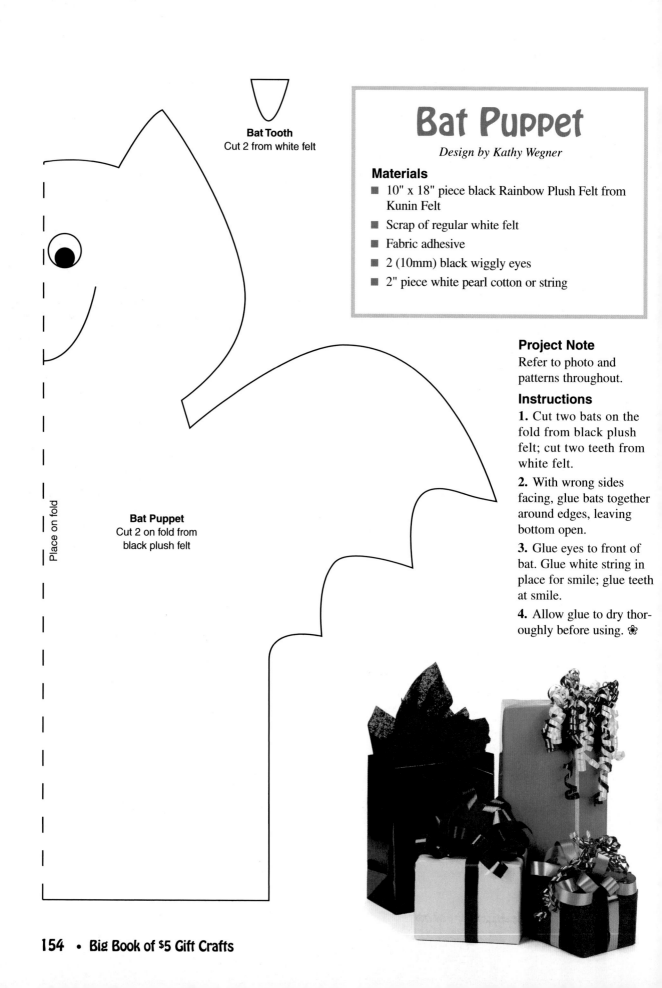

un puppets of plush felt require no sewing skills. They're simple enough to whip up in batches—what great favors for your child's Halloween party!

Jack-o'-Lantern Card

Design by Kathy Wegner

Materials

- 6½" x 5" blank black greeting card with envelope
- Paper Reflections paper products from DMD Industries Inc.: 5½" x 5" pieces orange and yellow corrugated papers; Green Creative Crinkle crinkled paper strips
- ¼" rectangular paper punch from Fiskars
- Spearmint #65313 Matte 3-D paint from Tulip
- Paper adhesive
- Tape
- Green thread or embroidery floss
- Hand-sewing needle

Those popular gel pens are just the ticket for adding a message to this vivid Halloween greeting.

Project Note

Refer to photo and pattern throughout.

Instructions

1. Cut jack-o'-lantern from yellow paper; do not cut out facial features. Cut another jack-o'-lantern from orange paper; trim out facial features.

2. On card front, punch two holes close together in each corner; pull four green crinkled paper strips through each pair of holes. Secure strips inside card with tape.

3. Glue orange jack-o'-lantern on top of yellow jack-o'-lantern. Paint jack-o'-lantern stem spearmint. When dry, bend two green paper strips into a bow shape; glue to jack-o'-lantern. Secure with a stitch or two of green thread.

4. Glue completed jack-o'-lantern to front of card. ❀

Jack-o'-Lantern Card
Cut 1 each from orange and yellow corrugated paper, cutting face from orange only

Save empty soup cans to make lots of these cute little treat totes. They make lovely favors for a Halloween or harvest party, too.

Project Notes

Refer to photo and patterns throughout.

Let all paints and ink dry between applications.

Cover any sharp edges inside can with masking tape or duct tape.

Instructions

1. Drill a hole in one corner of wooden square. Drill two holes in can opposite one another and ¼" below rim.

2. Paint exterior of can bright orange.

3. Using sea sponge, dab a little Sedona clay paint over bright orange using an up-and-down motion.

4. *Jack-o'-lantern face*: Position face on one side of can between holes at rim. Dab real red paint onto cheeks. Paint eyes, nose and mouth coal black. Using toothpick and bright white, add a highlight dot to top of each eye and three highlight dots to top of each cheek.

5. Using marking pen, write "Trick or Treat" on wooden square, positioning *Continued on page 162*

Pumpkin Treat Can

Design by Barbara Matthiessen

Materials

- Soup can, washed, dried and label removed
- 12" green fabric-covered stem wire
- No-Prep Metal Paints from DecoArt: coal black, bright orange, Sedona clay, bright white and real red
- Woodsies 1½" wooden square from Forster
- Ultra-fine-point black permanent marking pen
- 2" x 6" torn strip green checked fabric
- 20" piece jute twine
- Coordinating flat button
- Natural excelsior
- Craft drill with ½" bit
- Sea sponge
- Small paintbrush
- Toothpick

Spooky Spider Frame

Design by Mary Ayres

Materials

- 4" x 5" Pop-Up Paper frame
- 1¾" wooden disk from Forster
- 8 (⅝") wooden spools
- 2 (10mm) black round wiggly eyes
- 8 (5") pieces cut from fat black chenille stems
- 1" straw hat
- ¾" silk fall flower
- Orange satin ribbon: ⅜ yard ⅝", ¼ yard ¼"
- American acrylic paints from DecoArt: white wash #DA2, pumpkin #DA13, lavender #DA34, lamp black #DA67
- Paintbrushes: #6 and #8 round bristle, liner
- Fiskars ¹⁄₁₆" round hole punch
- Photo
- Tacky craft glue

Project Notes

Refer to photo and pattern throughout.

Let all paints dry between applications.

See directions for dry-brushing and rouging under "Painting Techniques" in the General Instructions on page 191.

Instructions

1. Using hole punch, punch holes down sides of frame where indicated by dots on pattern.

2. Paint all surfaces of disk (head), frame and spools lamp black. Dry-brush edges of disk, frame and spools with lavender.

3. Rouge cheeks on disk face with pumpkin. Paint mouth and cheek dots with white wash, using pointed end of brush handle dipped in paint for cheek dots. Glue wiggly eyes to head where indicated by dots on pattern.

4. Insert photo in frame.

5. Push ¼" of each chenille stem through a hole in side of frame from front to back; bend short end flat against back of frame to hold leg in place. Thread a spool on end of each stem for foot and bend ½" of stem end against back of spool to hold it in place. Bend legs up, then down in middle, and back up at spool feet.

6. Glue head to center top of frame. Tie ⅝" ribbon in a bow; notch ends and glue bow to head at center bottom.

7. Wrap ¼" ribbon around hat brim, overlapping ends on right side; glue. Trim ribbon ends ½" beyond overlap. Glue flower to right side of hat; glue hat to top of head on right side. Let dry. ✣

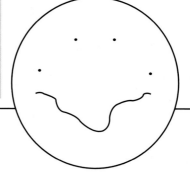

Spooky Spider Frame

Little ghouls and goblins will get a kick out of seeing their picture framed by this silly spider in a straw hat.

Crafting Tip
New Life for Dead Bolts

By Mary Ann Herman

Fabric-store clerks usually toss the empty fabric boards. Ask for a few. They can be covered with wallpaper or fabric and serve as lap boards, lightweight shelves or bulletin boards. Or cut into smaller pieces to use as hot-platter mats at the dining room table. Just put smaller piece on fabric, draw around it with a pencil. cut fabric with allowance for seams and height of fabric board, and speedily sew in pillowcase fashion to make it easy to remove, in case laundering is needed after that delicious banquet you served!

"Give Thanks" Banner

Design by Kathy Wegner

Materials

- Rainbow Felt Classic form Kunin: 2 (9" x 12") pieces mango tango, 9" x 12" piece each coral dawn, limbo lime, yellow, cashmere tan, cinnamon
- Fiskars scallop-edge shears
- 6-strand cotton embroidery floss: dark brown, tan
- Embroidery needle
- 7½" wooden strip or dowel
- Thick tacky craft glue
- Black permanent marker

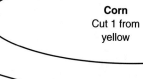

Corn
Cut 1 from
yellow

Husk
Cut 1 from
limbo lime

Pumpkin Stem
Cut 1 from
limbo lime

Apple
Cut 1 from
coral dawn

Project Notes

Refer to photo and patterns throughout.

Use regular scissors for cutting unless otherwise indicated.

Instructions

1. Cut letters and apple from coral dawn, cornucopia from cinnamon, corn from yellow, corn husk and pumpkin stem from limbo lime, and pumpkin from mango tango.

2. Using scallop-edge shears throughout, trim edges from second sheet of mango tango felt; trim sheet of cashmere tan felt to measure 7" x 10". From scraps of cashmere tan, use regular scissors to cut six ¼" x 12" strips of felt "raffia."

3. Pin cornucopia, pumpkin, corn with husk and apple to cashmere tan rectangle. Using 6 strands dark brown floss, sew all pieces to cashmere tan felt with long, irregular stitches. Using 2 strands tan floss, outline curl in cornucopia's tip with running stitch. Using 6 strands dark brown floss, sew cashmere tan panel to mango tango rectangle with long, irregular stitches.

4. Hold cashmere tan strips together; tie overhand knot in center. Using 6 strands tan floss, sew ends of strips to upper corners of mango tango felt panel. Trim ends of strips diagonally.

5. Glue letters to banner; glue pumpkin stem to pumpkin. Using marker, color in stem on apple. Glue dowel or wooden strip to back of banner along top. ✿

Patterns continued on page 162

Letters
Cut from
coral dawn

Beautiful autumn colors adorn this bright felt banner perfect for Thanksgiving.

Give thanks

"Give Thanks" Banner patterns continued from page 160

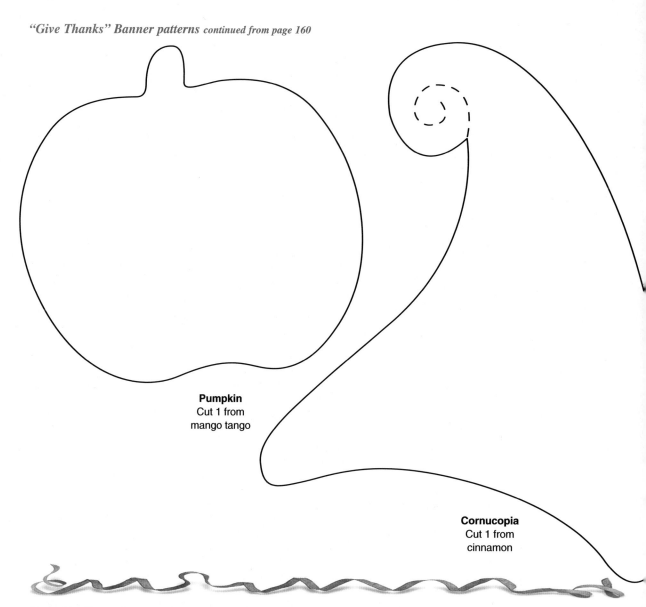

Pumpkin
Cut 1 from
mango tango

Cornucopia
Cut 1 from
cinnamon

Pumpkin Treat Can continued from page 157

hole in top corner; add squiggly outline.

6. *Handle:* Thread ends of stem wire through holes in can, leaving 2"–4" protruding outside can. Curl ends tightly around pencil.

7. Knot fabric strip around wire handle. Thread jute through hole in wooden square; tie in bow around fabric knot. Glue button to center of jute bow.

8. Fill can with excelsior. ❂

Pumpkin Treat Can Handle Decoration

Pumpkin Treat Can Face

marching down your table, or winging his way through the mail to a faraway friend, Pilgrim Tom brings Happy Thanksgiving greetings!

Pilgrim Turkey

Design by Missy Becker

Materials

- Wooden pieces: 5 (2") primitive hearts, ½" heart, 1¼" flowerpot, 1⅝" pigeon egg, 1¾" ball knob
- Americana acrylic paints from DecoArt: moon yellow #DA7, Georgia clay #DA17, sable brown #DA61, dark chocolate #DA65, lamp black #DA67, slate grey #DA68, light buttermilk #DA164, alizarin crimson #DA179, peony pink #DA215
- ⅔ yard ¼"-wide red satin ribbon
- Toothpick
- Cotton-tip swab
- Paintbrushes: #0 liner, #3 round, #8 shader
- Clear acrylic spray
- Transfer or graphite paper
- Sandpaper
- Wood glue and/or craft cement

Project Notes

Refer to photo and patterns throughout.

Refer to directions for base-coating, floating and shading under "Painting Techniques" in the General Instructions on page 191.

Refer to directions for transferring patterns under "Using Transfer & Graphite Paper" in the General Instructions on page 190.

Let all paints and sealer dry between applications.

Sanding & Painting

1. Sand bottom (broad end) of egg (head), and top and bottom of ball (body). Check to make sure that ball will not roll, and egg will sit on top of ball. Sand a flat area on back of ball where tail feathers will be attached.

2. Using shader and sable brown, paint body and primitive hearts (tail feathers).

3. Transfer vest pattern onto body. Paint vest and flowerpot (hat) slate grey; add ebony black hatband.

4. Using moon yellow, base-coat ½" heart (beak), 1¼" heart (feet) and hat buckle.

5. Paint remainder of body sable brown. Transfer wings and collar to vest; paint wings sable brown. Paint collar light buttermilk.

6. Working inward on tail feathers from curves toward points and using shader brush, float design first with alizarin crimson, then Georgia clay and last with dark chocolate.

7. Using dark chocolate, float shading on beak, feet, wings, around vest and hat buckle.

8. Transfer face to egg (head). Using round brush and lamp black throughout, paint eyes; float shading on vest and hat. Dot on buttons using handle of brush dipped in paint. Thin paint with water until it is the consistency of ink; using thinned mixture, line on eyelashes and stitching on collar.

9. Apply a little peony pink to cotton-tip swab; wipe off excess paint on a paper towel, then scrub cheeks in a circular motion, using swab like a stencil brush, to blush cheeks. *Continued on page 165.*

"Give Thanks" Plant Poke

Design by Carolyn V. Stearns

Materials

- Mini Innkeeper Garden Sign from Walnut Hollow
- ⅛" ribbon: 20" green, 20" yellow
- 18" ⅜" wired metallic gold ribbon
- Krylon Spray Gesso and Crystal Clear sealer
- ZIG 03 black Millennium Marker from EK Success Ltd.
- Americana acrylic paints from DecoArt: buttermilk #DA3, forest green #DA50, antique white #DA58, dark chocolate #DA65, brandy wine #DA79, Black Forest green #DA83, raw sienna #DA93, rookwood red #DA97, honey brown #DA163, golden straw #DA168, marigold #DA194
- Paintbrushes: ¾" wash, #12 shader, #1, #3 and #6, #0 liner
- Stylus
- Transfer paper
- Fine sandpaper
- Tack cloth

Project Notes

Refer to photo and pattern throughout.

Let all paints, ink, gesso and sealer dry between applications.

See instructions for transferring design under "Using Transfer & Graphite Paper" in General Instructions on page 190.

Instructions

1. Sand sign; wipe with tack cloth. Spray with gesso.

2. Paint sign and stick marigold; shade edges of sign with honey brown.

3. Transfer turkey and lettering to sign. Paint head and tummy antique white; shade with honey brown. Paint collar buttermilk; shade with marigold. Paint hat dark chocolate and hatband with golden straw.

4. Using stylus, add tiny black dots for eyes; add very tiny highlight dots of antique white.

5. Paint beak golden straw; paint wattle brandy wine.

6. Beginning at bottom left, paint feathers in order: forest green shaded with Black Forest green; brandy wine shaded with rookwood red; raw sienna shaded with dark chocolate; golden straw shaded with honey brown. Repeat till all feathers are painted. Shade around turkey feathers with honey brown.

7. Paint lettering forest green; add dots at ends of letters with stylus dipped in forest green paint.

8. Add outlines and other details with black marker.

9. Spray with two or three coats of clear sealer.

10. Holding all ribbons together, tie in bow around stick at base of turkey. Twirl ends of wired ribbon around paintbrush handle; trim ribbon ends as desired. ❆

Dress up the simplest green plant with this colorful plant poke painted in the rich colors of an autumn harvest.

"Give Thanks" Plant Poke

Pilgrim Turkey continued from page 163

10. Using toothpick dipped in light buttermilk, dot highlights onto eyes and cheeks. Thin paint to an inky consistency and add highlight lines to eyes.

Finishing & Assembly

1. Glue tail feathers together side by side in a fan shape. Glue head to body and body to feet.

2. *Wattle & beak:* Fold ribbon in half; trim ribbon ends in rounded shape. Glue fold to back of beak (½" heart) and glue beak on head.

3. Glue hat onto head; glue tail feathers to back of body.

4. Spray turkey with a coat or two of acrylic spray. ✿

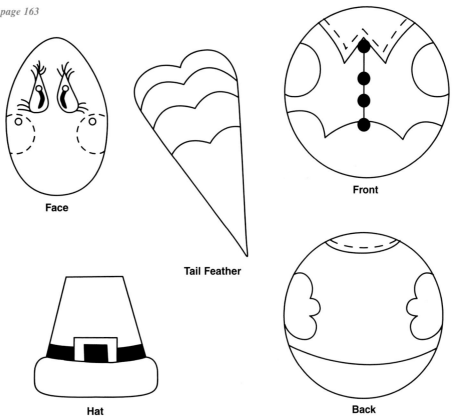

Face

Tail Feather

Front

Hat

Back

Merry Christmas

ount your blessings, because with this collection of merry crafts, you won't have to do any Christmas shopping! You're sure to find just the right holiday surprise for everyone on your gift list with this festive collection of Christmas gifts and decorations!

Teddy Mitten Ornament

Design by Barbara Matthiessen

Materials

- 1 child's mitten
- ¼ sheet light brown craft foam
- 2" white wooden snowflake
- Assorted *torn* fabric scraps: 1¼" x 10", 2" x 8", 2 small square patches
- 2 flat 2-hole or 4-hole buttons
- Fabric glue
- ZIG markers from EK Success Ltd.: brown and red pigment ink markers, 05 black marker
- Black embroidery floss and hand-sewing needle
- Polyester fiberfill
- Stiff fabric brush or stencil brush
- Graphite paper

Project Notes

Refer to photo and patterns throughout.

Refer to directions for transferring patterns under "Using Transfer & Graphite Paper" in the General Instructions on page 190.

Instructions

1. From light brown craft foam, cut one base, one head and two paws using long, smooth scissors strokes and turning the foam as you cut.

2. Transfer details onto head and paws as needed using graphite paper.

3. Shade edges of paws and head with brown pigment marker, running the marker along the edge for a few inches and then brushing the still-wet ink toward the center with a stiff brush.

4. Using the black marker, draw wiggly outlines around head and paws; fill in eyes and nose. Rub brush on end of red marker; color cheeks by dabbing brush using an up-and-down motion. Fill in tongue with red marker.

5. Stuff mitten lightly with fiberfill. Insert flat end of base into mitten so that point protrudes ¾" beyond mitten cuff. Glue bear head to point of base. Glue snowflake to front of mitten ¾" from top. Glue paws to mitten, placing tops under bottom edge of head and positioning left paw to cover top of one snowflake point.

6. Glue small fabric patches to front of mitten.

7. *Hanger:* Tie an overhand knot in the center of the 2" x 8" fabric strip. Twist sides of strip, then insert ends into mitten and glue in place. Glue top of mitten closed. Tie 1¼" x 10" strip in a bow around center of handle.

8. Thread floss through holes in buttons, knotting floss with floss ends on front; trim floss ends. Glue one button to patches and one to center of bow on handle. ✿

Paw
Cut 2 from light brown craft foam

Patterns continued on page 173

Use up those odd mittens with this fun and friendly project! It's adorable hanging on your tree or dangling from a doorknob.

**hat goes 'Arf, arf, Merry Christmas'?"**
Remember that silly riddle from
childhood? Give it a sweet face with this sculpted seal pup.

Project Notes

Refer to manufacturer's instructions for working with modeling compound; condition it as directed before molding pieces.

Refer to photo and patterns throughout.

Instructions

1. *Body:* Roll a ¾" ball of white; roll into a cylinder that is slightly narrower at one end; flatten smaller end and shape as shown in Fig. 1.

2. *Front flippers:* Roll two ¼" balls of white; roll each into a teardrop shape. Flatten them slightly and press narrow ends onto front (rounded end) of body, bending out flippers as shown.

3. *Head:* Roll ⅝" ball of white; referring to Fig. 2, press two black seed beads into head for eyes. For snout, roll two ⅛" balls of white; flatten each slightly and press onto face side by side, below eyes. For nose, roll a tiny ball of black slightly smaller than the seed beads and press into center of snout.

4. *Hat:* Roll a ¾" ball of red. Form into hat shape referring to Fig. 3. Press hat onto top of head, bending tip to one side. Roll a ⅜" ball of white; press onto tip of hat. Roll ½" ball of white; roll ball into a thin rope and flatten until it is ¼" wide. Wrap around base of hat, starting and ending in back

and trimming off excess modeling compound.

5. Using toothpick or straight edge, gently press two eyelashes alongside each eye; using tip of toothpick, press round indentations into snout. Rub a little blush on cheeks with the tip of your little finger.

6. Break ½" off one end of toothpick; press ¼" into upper body; press head onto other end.

7. Set seal on an ovenproof plate and bake in a preheated oven at 265 degrees Fahrenheit for 20 minutes. Let cool.

8. Using tip of paintbrush handle dipped in white paint, dot hat randomly with spots. ✖

Christmas Seal

Design by Becky Meverden

Materials

- Premo! Sculpey modeling compound from Polyform Products: white #5001, black #5042, cadmium red #5382
- Craft knife
- 2 (2mm) black seed beads
- Pink cosmetic blusher
- White acrylic paint
- Small paintbrush
- Round toothpick
- Ovenproof plate

Fig. 2

Fig. 1   **Fig. 3**

From trash to treasure, empty tin cans are transformed into charming containers for treats and small gifts.

Recycled Gift Tins

Design by Ann Butler

Materials

- Empty can, washed and dried (see Project Notes)
- Krylon Interior/Exterior paint in color(s) of your choice
- White acrylic paint
- Old toothbrush
- Fabric of your choice with holiday motifs
- Pinking shears (optional)
- 12" 19-gauge craft wire
- Hammer and large nail
- Needle-nose pliers
- Craft glue
- Small paintbrush

Project Notes

Refer to photo throughout. Sample projects were made using a small tuna can, 1½" high and 3¼" in diameter, and a rectangular can from powdered coffee mix, 4⅛" wide x 2⅝" deep x 2½" high.

Let all coats of paint and glue dry between applications.

Instructions

1. Spray interior of can with two coats interior/exterior paint. Turn can upside down and spray outside with two or three coats, using same color or contrasting color as desired.

2. Using pinking shears or scissors as desired, cut fabric motifs to fit on side of can. Glue fabric in place.

3. Using hammer and nail, punch two holes in can opposite each other for fastening handle.

4. Place can with bottom up. Dip toothbrush in white acrylic paint; holding brush 12"–18" from can, pull finger or craft stick across bristles to spatter can.

5. Thread wire ends through holes, adjusting handle length as desired. Wrap excess wire around handle, curling it and twisting ends with needle-nose pliers.

6. Tear or cut a strip of matching or complementary fabric; tie around wire handle. ❈

 **little paint, scraps of felt and a few wooden cutouts are all it takes to transform tiny flowerpots into sweet Yuletide favors!**

Project Notes

Refer to photo throughout.

Allow all paints, ink and finish to dry between applications.

Santa

1. Invert saucer; glue to bottom of pot.

2. Paint flowerpot rim and saucer true red; paint remainder of pot's exterior white wash.

3. For face, draw 1¼" circle just below red pot rim; paint circle base flesh.

4. Using craft knife, cut large wooden circle in half for mustache halves; paint white wash on all surfaces. Paint furniture plug shading flesh (nose), and small wooden circle lamp black (button).

5. Using marking pen, outline each mustache piece with "running stitch." Glue nose and mustache to face; glue button to saucer. Dip stylus in lamp black; touch to face for eyes. In same manner, add a single true red dot for mouth, and two white

wash dots to button for holes. Add straight eyebrows with marking pen.

6. Spray all surfaces with two or three coats of matte finish.

7. Glue ¼" strip of felt around neck and ⅜" strip around lower portion of pot rim, trimming ends and butting them together in back.

Snowman

1. Invert saucer; glue to bottom of pot.

2. Paint flowerpot rim lamp black; paint remainder of pot and saucer white wash.

3. Paint teardrop tangelo orange (nose); paint all surfaces of holly leaves holly green and circle true
Continued on page 181

Santa & Snowman Candy Cups

Designs by Chris Malone

Materials

Each Candy Cup

- 2¼" terra-cotta flowerpot with saucer
- Paintbrush and stylus
- Black fine-line permanent marking pen
- Krylon Spray Matte Finish
- Craft cement

Santa

- Woodsies wooden cutouts from Forster: large (1¼") circle, small (⅜") circle
- ¼" wooden furniture plug
- Craft knife
- Americana acrylic paints from DecoArt: white wash #DA2, lamp black #DA67, true red #DA129, base flesh #DA136, shading flesh #DA137
- White Rainbow Plush Felt from Kunin: ¼" x 5¼" and ⅜" x 8" strips

Snowman

- Woodsies wooden cutouts from Forster: large (1½") teardrop, 2 medium (1¼") holly leaves, small (⅜") circle
- Americana acrylic paints from DecoArt: white wash #DA2, holly green #DA48, bright green #DA54, lamp black #DA67, true red #DA129, tangelo orange #DA196
- Small stencil brush
- 10" x ¾" strip lime Rainbow Felt Classic from Kunin
- 1⅞" x 6½" strip black corrugated paper

Mittens Banner & Garland

Designs by Debra Quartermain

Materials

Both Projects

- Rainbow Felt Classic from Kunin: 1 yard each hunter green and navy, 1⅛ yards ruby, 2 (9" x 12") sheets white
- Cotton embroidery floss: white and burgundy
- Embroidery needle
- White sewing thread
- Plaid paints: white acrylic and white pearl dimensional fabric paint
- 2½" snowflake stamp from Back Street
- 1" foam brush
- Small paintbrush
- 14" ¼"-diameter wooden dowel
- Polyester fiberfill
- 3 yards craft wire
- 1 yard fusible web
- Fabric glue
- Sewing machine or hand-sewing needle
- Straight pins

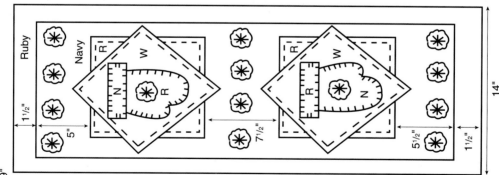

Fig. 1
R-Ruby
N-Navy
W-White

Project Notes

Refer to photo, pattern and Fig. 1 throughout.

All blanket stitch and running stitch is done with 6 strands of floss. Separate floss strands and recombine them without twisting before stitching.

Refer to manufacturer's instructions for using fusible web.

Banner

1. From navy felt, cut one piece 13" x 36", one mitten, and one piece 2" x 5" for mitten cuff. From ruby felt, cut one piece 14" x 39", two 9" squares, one mitten, one piece 2" x 5" for mitten cuff and one piece 2" x 12" for hanger strip. From white felt, cut two 9" squares.

Warm up your holiday interiors with these home-decor accents crafted from felt in deep, rich colors.

2. Lay hanger strip across back of ruby 14" x 39" panel, centering it from side to side and positioning top edge of strip about 1¾" below top of large panel. Pin in place and, by hand or machine, sew strip to large panel along long edges, leaving ends open for inserting hanging rod later.

3. Referring to Fig. 1, pin ruby mitten to white square on the diagonal; pin navy mitten cuff in place so that it overlaps mitten by ¼". Using white floss and ¼" stitches, blanket-stitch mitten and cuff to white felt.

4. Repeat step 3 with navy mitten, ruby cuff and white felt square, reversing mitten before stitching.

5. Apply fusible web to back of 13" x 36" navy panel; center navy panel on front of ruby panel and fuse in place. Fuse ruby

squares to navy felt; secure with white running stitch around edges. Fuse white squares on top of ruby squares on the diagonal; secure with burgundy running stitch around edges.

6. *Snowflakes:* Brush a thin layer of white acrylic paint on snowflake rubber stamp and stamp onto remaining piece of navy felt. Leaving sufficient space between snowflakes to cut them out, repeat to stamp a total of 14 snowflakes. Define center of each snowflake with white pearl dimensional paint. When paints are completely dry, cut out each snowflake. Using fabric glue, glue snowflake to center of each mitten, and in rows of four at top, center and bottom of banner.

7. Slip dowel through casing on back of banner and hang as desired.

Garland

1. From navy felt, cut two mittens and four pieces 2" x 5" for mitten cuffs. From ruby felt, cut four mittens and two pieces 2" x 5" for mitten cuffs. From hunter green, cut four strips 4" x 36".

2. Lay two forest green felt strips on top of each other, matching edges. By hand or machine, sew a ⅜"-wide casing down center. Repeat with remaining forest green strips.

3. Fringe felt pieces on each side of casing, making cuts ¼" apart and cutting from edge up to—but not *through*—stitching. Thread wire through casings in fringed felt; gather to 30" long. Twist extra wire at each end to make a hanging loop.

4. Pin a ruby mitten cuff to each navy mitten, reversing one, so that cuff overlaps mitten by ¼"; repeat with navy

cuffs and ruby mittens, reversing two. Using white floss, blanket-stitch cuff edge that overlaps mitten. Pin matching mittens together in pairs and blanket-stitch around edges, leaving tops open. Stuff mittens lightly with fiberfill.

5. Tack ruby mittens to ends of garland with thumbs facing in; tack navy mitten in center.

6. Referring to step 6 for banner, make a total of seven snowflakes. Glue a snowflake to front of each mitten, and pairs of snowflakes to garland between mittens, spacing them evenly. ❄

Mitten
For banner, cut 1 each
from navy and ruby
For garland, cut 2
from navy and 4 from ruby

Teddy Mitten Ornament *continued from page 168*

Base
Cut 1 from light brown craft foam

Head
Cut 1 from light brown craft foam

An embossed papier-mâché box gives this project a positively opulent look! Fill it with treats for gift giving, or simply enjoy its colorful design on your buffet or coffee table.

Project Notes
Refer to photo throughout.

Let all coats of paint and ink dry between applications.

See directions for dry-brushing and stenciling under "Painting Techniques" in the General Instructions on page 191.

Instructions
1. Paint exterior of box (not lid) with mistletoe; dry-brush surface with emperor's gold.

2. Paint sides and top of lid with antique white. Tape wreath stencil to center of lid. Stencil bow with country red; shade edges with emperor's gold. Stencil holly leaves with mistletoe; shade edges with dark pine. Stencil holly berries with country red. Stencil gingerbread men with honey brown; shade edges with light cinnamon. Stencil stars with emperor's gold.

3. Reposition stencil for embellishments on gingerbread men. Stencil buttons with lamp black; stencil bands of icing with emperor's gold.

Stenciled Christmas Box
Design by Mary Ayres

Materials
- 8" round papier-mâché box with lid with embossed poinsettias on the side from JoAnn Stores
- ¾ yard ¾"-wide red fabric ribbon
- ⅝" red flat button
- Simply Stencils wreath #28853 from Plaid
- Americana acrylic paints from DecoArt: country red #DA18, dark pine #DA49, mistletoe #DA53, antique white #DA58, lamp black #DA67, light cinnamon #DA114, honey brown #DA163
- Emperor's gold #DA148 Dazzling Metallics acrylic paint from DecoArt
- Paintbrushes: 2 #8 round bristle brushes, ¼" stencil brush for each color of paint
- ZIG Memory System markers from EK Success Ltd.: extra-fine-tip opaque gold permanent writer, fine-tip black permanent marker
- Sticky Dots adhesive from Therm O Web
- Masking tape

4. Using emperor's gold, stencil stars randomly around wreath on lid.

5. Using black marker, outline bow, holly leaves and berries, gingerbread men and stars with dotted lines. Using gold writer, add a dot to center of each berry, and draw dotted lines coming out from indentations in stars.

6. Wrap ribbon around side of box lid; trim to fit. Using Sticky Dots, adhere ribbon to lid, butting ends of ribbon together at top of design. Using adhesive dot, adhere button to side of lid over ribbon ends. ❈

Here's the perfect presentation for home-made holiday treats, an ideal collection spot for Christmas cards.

Snowflake Basket & Ornament

Designs by Mary Ayres

Materials

Both Projects

- Market basket
- 2 (3") wooden snowflake cutouts from Darice
- 1 yard 1½"-wide white Battenburg lace
- 10" piece silver pearl cotton
- Simply Stencils snowflake stencil #28191 from Plaid
- Americana acrylic paints from DecoArt: true blue #DA36, country blue #DA41
- Shimmering silver #DA70 Dazzling Metallics acrylic paint from DecoArt
- Paintbrushes: #6 and #8 rounds, ¼" stencil brush
- ZIG twin-tip blue permanent Memory System writer from EK Success Ltd.
- Tacky craft glue
- Craft drill and ³⁄₃₂" bit
- Fine sandpaper

Project Notes

Refer to photo throughout.

Sample basket measures 8½" long x 5" wide and 7" tall, but a basket of any size may be used.

See directions for dry-brushing under "Painting Techniques" in the General Instructions on page 191.

Let all paints and inks dry between applications.

Basket

1. Paint all surfaces of basket true blue. Dry-brush exterior with country blue.

2. Using shimmering silver paint and stencil brush, stencil snowflakes around sides of basket in each of the overlapped sections. Stencil circle in center of each snowflake with true blue; stencil zigzag line across center top of basket handle with shimmering silver.

3. Glue lace around basket, butting ends together at center of handle.

4. Lightly sand snowflake. Paint shimmering silver and dry-brush edges with true blue. Stencil a true blue circle in the center of each point of snowflake.

5. Write "Happy Holidays" in center of snowflake with fine tip of blue marker; add dots at ends of letters using bullet tip.

6. Glue snowflake to side of basket to cover bottom of handle and ends of lace.

Ornament

1. In remaining snowflake, drill a hole in the center of one point.

2. Complete steps 4 and 5 as for basket.

3. Thread pearl cotton through hole in snowflake and knot ends for hanging loop. ❀

This ornament cone bears a special guest—a frosty visitor with a halo of greenery.

Project Notes

Refer to photo and pattern throughout.

See instructions for floating under "Painting Techniques" in the General Instructions on page 191.

Let all paints and glue dry between applications.

Instructions

1. Paint ball knob (head) titanium white and furniture plug (nose) pumpkin.

2. Dip cotton-tip swab into peony pink; rub off excess paint onto paper towel. With swab, "scrub" cheeks onto head in a circular motion.

3. Using round brush and lamp black paint, paint eyes. Thin a little lamp black paint to an inky consistency with water; using liner, add mouth and eyelashes with thinned mixture. Dipping toothpick into mixture, add dot to each end of mouth.

4. Using shader, float a shadow of Georgia clay onto one edge of nose.

5. Using a toothpick dipped in titanium white, add single highlight dots to each eye and top edge of each cheek.

6. Run paper circle through paper crimper to replicate markings on an ice-cream cone, if desired. Fold circle into a cone shape; secure with glue; V-shaped notch will be at center front. For hanger, glue ends of cord inside cone on opposite sides.

7. Glue snowman head into cone; glue plug nose to face.

8. Make halo out of pine garland; glue to head. Glue red beads to front of wreath in a cluster to look like berries.

9. Apply snow paste around rim of cone and down V of cone in front to make collar and fill in empty areas; dab a little snow paste onto halo.

10. Thread white floss through buttonholes; knot on front and trim ends. Glue button to center front of cone. ❦

Snowcone Snowman

Snowcone Snowman Ornament

Design by Missy Becker

Materials

- 1¼" wooden ball knob
- ¼" wooden furniture plug
- 5" piece miniature pine garland
- 3 (4mm) metallic red beads
- ½" flat green button
- White embroidery floss
- 3" circle cut from heavy brown paper
- Paper crimper (optional)
- Americana acrylic paints from DecoArt: titanium white #DA1, pumpkin #DA13, Georgia clay #DA17, lamp black #DA67, peony pink #DA215
- DecoArt Snow-Tex #DAS9 snow paste
- Paintbrushes: #0 liner, #3 round, #8 shader
- 7" metallic gold fine cord
- Tacky craft glue
- Cotton-tip swab
- Toothpick

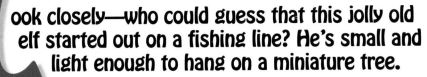

Santa Bobber Ornament

Design by Missy Becker

Materials

- Round plastic fishing bobber with white top and red bottom
- ¼" wooden furniture plug
- 1" wooden heart cutout
- ³⁄₁₆"–¼" red jingle bell
- 1" piece miniature holly garland
- 2" piece white fuzzy chenille stem
- 8" piece green embroidery floss
- Americana acrylic paints from DecoArt: titanium white #DA1, lamp black #DA67, flesh tone #DA78, Delane's cheek color #DA182
- Paintbrushes: #0 liner, #5 round, #8 shader
- Tacky craft glue
- Toothpick

Project Notes

Refer to photo and pattern throughout.

See instructions for floating under "Painting Techniques" in the General Instructions on page 191.

Let all paints and glue dry between applications.

Instructions

1. Using shader and flesh tone paint throughout, paint a half-circle face on white side of bobber, and paint furniture plug (nose).

2. Using lamp black throughout, paint eyes and all surfaces of heart cutout (shoes). Add water to a little paint to make a mixture of an inky consistency; using liner, add a narrow "belt" around bobber between red and white sections; add eyelashes.

3. Using Delane's cheek color throughout, float cheeks onto face below eyes and float shading along bottom of furniture plug.

4. Thin a little titanium white to an inky consistency; using liner, add highlight strokes to eyes. Using toothpick, add a single highlight dot to eyes at top of each highlight stroke; add also a single highlight dot along top edge of each cheek, and a series of three highlight dots along unshaded edge of nose.

5. Knot floss ends to make loop. Depress button on top of bobber to expose copper wire; hook loop onto wire and release button.

6. Glue shoes to bottom of bobber (point to back) and nose to face. Coil fuzzy chenille stem into a flat circle and glue under nose. Glue a leaf or two from holly garland at top of head by button; glue jingle bell over leaves for berry. ❀

Santa Bobber Ornament

Holiday Chalkboard Duo

Designs by Mary Ayres

Materials

Each Project

- Fine sandpaper
- Graphite or transfer paper
- Tacky craft glue

Gingerbread Lady

- 5¾" x 7¾" chalkboard with wooden frame
- Wooden cutouts from Lara's Crafts: 4" x 7" angel, 5 (¾") hearts
- Americana acrylic paints from DecoArt: country

red #DA18, mistletoe #DA53, light cinnamon #DA114, honey brown #DA163

- Glorious gold #DA71 Dazzling Metallics acrylic paint from DecoArt
- Paintbrushes: #6 and #8 round bristles, ¼" stencil
- Simply Stencils checkerboard stencil #29624 from Plaid
- ZIG Memory System markers from EK Success Ltd.: black twin-tip permanent marker, extra-fine-tip white opaque writer
- ¼ yard ⅜" wired gold ribbon

Choose a gingerbread lady or frosty snow angel and dress up your decor with these country-style chalkboards.

Project Notes

Refer to photo and patterns throughout.

See directions for dry-brushing and rouging under "Painting Techniques" in the General Instructions on page 191.

See directions for transferring patterns under "Using Transfer & Graphite Paper" in General Instructions on page 190.

Let all paints and inks dry between applications.

Gingerbread Lady

1. Sand wooden pieces lightly as needed. Paint angel (gingerbread lady) honey brown; dry-brush edges with light cinnamon.

2. Transfer eye, chest and cheek dots to lady. Rouge cheeks with country red. Using side of black marker's bullet tip, add eye dots and buttons. Using white writer, add single highlight dot to each cheek and dot-dash outlines.

3. Paint chalkboard frame mistletoe. Leaving corners of frame blank, stencil a single row of squares along each of the four sides with glorious gold. Using black marker's fine tip, outline stenciled squares and the mistletoe spaces between them with short dashed lines.

4. Transfer words to chalkboard; go over them with white writer.

5. Paint hearts country red; dry-brush edges with glorious gold.

6. Glue gingerbread lady to frame; glue one heart to lady and remaining hearts in frame's corners with heart points pointing toward center. Tie gold ribbon in a bow; trim ends and glue bow to lady's neckline.

Snow Angel

1. Sand wooden pieces lightly as needed. Paint snowman and wings antique white; paint wings again with oyster pearl. Paint teardrop (nose) gingerbread.

Dry-brush all edges with Mississippi mud.

2. Transfer eye and mouth dots to snowman. Rouge cheeks with country red. Using brown marker, add

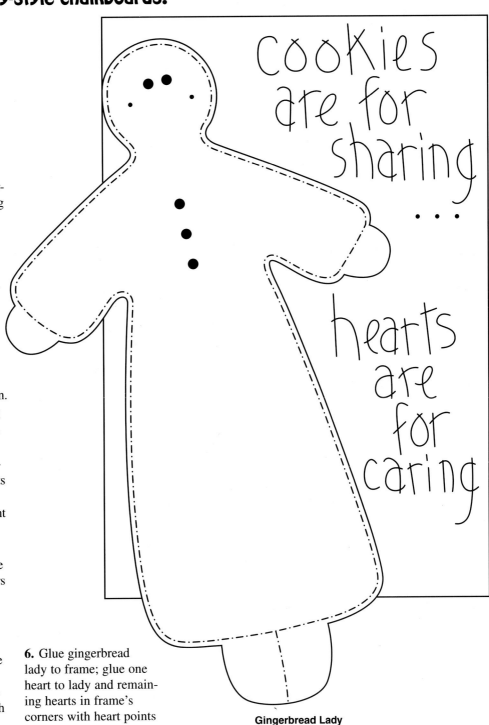

cookies are for sharing . . .

hearts are for caring

Gingerbread Lady

eyes and mouth and dashed lines around edges of snowman, wings and nose.

3. Glue wings to back of snowman and teardrop nose to face. Glue buttons evenly spaced down front.

4. Paint bottom section of frame antique white; paint remainder of frame Williamsburg blue. Dry-brush outer edges of frame with Mississippi mud. Using brown marker, draw short dashed lines around antique white section, and around edges of Williamsburg blue sections, including edges

adjacent to antique white section.

5. Transfer words and snowflakes to chalkboard and add four more snowflakes to frame. Go over them with white writer.

6. Paint stars olde gold; dry-brush edges with Mississippi mud.

7. Glue snowman and wings to chalkboard. Glue stars onto frame. ✿

Snow Angel

- 6¾" x 8¾" chalkboard with wooden frame
- Wooden cutouts from Darice: 3" x 4" wings, 2" x 6" snowman
- ⅞" Woodsies wooden teardrop from Forster
- 3 (1") wooden stars
- 3 (⅜") flat white buttons
- Americana acrylic paints from DecoArt: country red #DA18, Williamsburg blue #DA40, antique white #DA58, Mississippi mud #DA94, olde gold #DA176, gingerbread #DA218
- Oyster pearl #DA203 Dazzling Metallics acrylic paint from DecoArt
- Paintbrushes: #6 and #8 round bristles, #6 soft round
- ZIG Memory System markers from EK Success Ltd.: brown fine-tip permanent marker, extra-fine-tip white opaque writer

Snow falls, the stars peek out

Snow angels gather bout

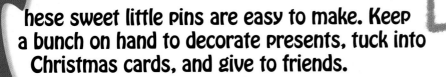

These sweet little pins are easy to make. Keep a bunch on hand to decorate presents, tuck into Christmas cards, and give to friends.

Mini Stick Snowman Pin

Design by Missy Becker

Materials

Each Pin

- Mini craft stick
- Wooden toothpick
- Americana acrylic paints from DecoArt: titanium white #DA1, #DA13, lamp black #DA67, peony pink #DA215
- Small paintbrush
- Cotton-tip swab
- 1½" square cut from ribbing or lightweight sock
- Embroidery floss in color to match sock for bow tie, and in contrasting color for hat trim
- 1" pin back
- Tacky craft glue
- Hot-glue gun

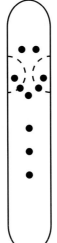

Mini Stick Snowman Pin

Project Notes

Refer to photo and pattern throughout.

Use tacky glue unless instructed otherwise.

Let all paints and glues dry between applications.

Instructions

1. Paint all surfaces of craft stick titanium white. Paint half of toothpick pumpkin; clip or break off ½"–¾" from painted end for nose. Touch up cut end with pumpkin.

2. Dip swab in peony pink paint; rub off most of paint onto paper towel, then use swab to "scrub" cheeks in a circular motion to rouge them as desired.

3. Glue nose to face at an angle.

4. Using other end of toothpick dipped in black paint, dot on eyes, mouth and buttons.

5. *Bow tie:* Using floss to match hat fabric, tie a small bow and glue to snowman below mouth and above top button.

6. *Hat:* Hot-glue one edge of fabric square to back of stick, turning up about ³⁄₁₆"–¼" along bottom to make hat cuff; then stretch fabric around to back of stick and hot-glue in place. Tie a length of contrasting floss around hat about ⅜" below top edge; knot tightly on front to close top of hat; trim floss ends evenly.

7. Glue pin back to back of snowman. ❀

Santa & Snowman Candy Cups continued from page 171

red (holly berry).

4. Using stencil brush, lightly tap bright green around edges of leaves. Clean brush. Combine a little white wash and true red to make pink. Dip stencil brush into mixture; tap off excess paint onto paper towel. Tap brush onto center section of flowerpot to make two cheeks.

5. Dip stylus in lamp black; touch to face for eyes and mouth. In same manner, add a single white wash dot to berry for highlight. Using marking pen throughout, add straight eyebrows and "running stitch" outlines around nose and leaves.

6. Glue nose to face; glue holly leaves and berry to rim (hat brim).

7. Spray all surfaces with two or three coats of matte finish.

8. Snip short ends of felt strip (scarf) to make fringe; wrap around neck and knot at one side. Roll up corrugated paper and insert in pot. ❀

Snowman Sock Ornament

Design by Veleta Stafney

Materials

- 3 white tube socks in newborn's size (0–6 months)
- ¼" round wooden furniture plug
- Americana acrylic paints from DecoArt: titanium white #DA1, lamp black #DA67, tangelo orange #DA196
- Pink powdered cosmetic blusher
- Small paintbrush
- Cotton-tip swab
- Stylus or toothpick
- Polyester fiberfill
- Hand-sewing needle and white thread
- 2" black felt hat
- Red-and-black checked fabric: 1" x 8¾" strip, 3 (⅝") squares
- Flat white buttons: ½", 2 (⅜")
- 3" candy cane
- ¼ yard fine gold cord
- Fabric glue

f you've ever been socked in by a snowstorm, here's your chance to get even! This sweet little guy is constructed from newborn-size white socks!

Project Note

Refer to photo throughout.

Instructions

1. *Body:* Cut cuff from one sock and discard. Sew basting stitch along raw edge; stuff sock semi-firmly with fiberfill; pull gathers tight and knot.

2. *Head:* Thread needle with long double length of thread; knot ends. Attach needle 1½" down from center of toe edge of body. Wrap thread around sock twice; pull thread tight to indent and knot.

3. *Legs:* Cut cuff from one sock and discard. From raw edge, cut one 1½" piece; set aside for one arm. Sew basting stitch along raw edge. Stuff semi-firmly, pull gathers tight, and knot. For feet, connect thread 1" from center of toe seam. Wrap thread twice around leg, pulling thread tight to indent and knot. Repeat to make a second leg.

4. *Attach legs:* Insert needle 1" above bottom of body through one side of body to other side, then through one leg. Insert needle back through same leg, through body and through other leg. Repeat twice, pulling thread tight. Insert needle through one leg and bring needle out between leg and body; knot thread.

5. *Arms:* Sew basting stitch along one raw edge of one arm piece. Pull thread tight and knot. Sew basting stitch along other raw edge; pull gathers tight and stuff semi-firmly. For hands, connect thread ½" from one raw edge. Wrap thread twice around arm, pulling tight to indent, and knot. Attach arms to body in same manner as legs.

6. *Face:* Paint furniture plug tangelo orange for nose; when dry, glue to face area. Using rounded end of paintbrush, paint two lamp black dots for eyes and one for mouth. Using stylus dipped in titanium white, add comma stroke to nose. Blush cheeks with cotton-tip swab dipped in cosmetic blusher.

7. Glue hat to head. Thread large-eye needle with gold cord and take a small stitch in top of hat; remove needle and knot ends; trim. Unravel all four sides of fabric strip and squares. Wrap strip around neck off to side. Glue one fabric square to hat and two down center of body. Glue larger button to square on hat and smaller buttons to squares on body. Glue candy cane in one hand. ❀

Welcome the winter holidays with this delightful ornament. Hang it in a window, or suspend it from a drawer pull or doorknob.

Tin-Punch Snowman Ornament

Design by Sandra Graham Smith

Materials

- Wide-mouth gold canning jar lid with blank, flat top
- Glossy enamel paints: white, red, black, brown, green, orange
- Small artist paintbrush
- Toothpick
- Black fine-line permanent marker
- 4"-diameter white paper lace doily
- Red felt
- Black 6-strand embroidery floss and large-eye needle
- Tacky craft glue
- Pinking shears
- Pressed-wood board or other hard, protective surface
- Hammer
- Several finishing nails
- Tracing paper
- Masking tape

Project Notes

Refer to photo and patterns throughout.

Let paints and ink dry between applications.

Painted Ornament

1. Trace pattern for snowman onto tracing paper. Cut out. Tape pattern on right side of lid.

2. Place lid on protective surface. Use hammer to tap nail from dot to dot, piercing tin. Change nail when point dulls.

3. Hold up punched lid to light; repunch any holes where necessary. Remove pattern and tape. Smooth side will be front.

4. Paint designs inside punched lines using thick strokes: *white*—snowman head and body sections; *red*—birdhouse, earmuffs and scarf; *brown*—stick arms; *black*—birdhouse roof and earmuffs band.

5. Paint orange carrot nose on snowman's face. Using liner brush and green paint, add stripes to red scarf.

6. Using black marker, add fringe to ends of scarf; dot on two eyes and smaller dots to form mouth; add detail to nose.

Finishing

1. Using pinking shears, cut 4¼" circle from red felt.

2. Glue paper doily to center of felt; glue punched, painted ornament to center of doily.

3. Thread hanging loop of black embroidery floss through felt and doily at center top of ornament. ❧

Tin-Punch Snowman

Felt Pattern
Cut 1 from felt with pinking shears

Stained Glass Tree Trims

Designs by Bonnie Lester

Materials

Each Ornament

- 2½" round clear glass ornament
- Glass from 8" x 10" picture frame
- Paintbrushes
- Toothpicks

Poinsettia

- Gold Glitter #16122 Liquid Leading from Plaid
- Gallery Glass window colors from Plaid: crystal clear #16001, ruby red #16015
- 3 (10mm) gemstones in color of your choice

Candy Stripe

- Silver Glitter #16123 Liquid Leading from Plaid
- Gallery Glass window colors from Plaid: kelly green #16008, white pearl #16021
- Single-edge razor blade or craft knife

Starburst

- Gold Glitter #16122 Liquid Leading from Plaid
- White pearl #16021 Gallery Glass window color from Plaid
- Clear 10mm gemstone
- Narrow-mouth cup or glass to use as work stand

Project Notes

Refer to photo and patterns throughout. Read following instructions for "Applying Leading" and "Applying Colors" before beginning work on individual designs.

Refer to manufacturer's instructions for using leading and window colors. Where leading spreads too wide or runs together, let it stand for five to 10 minutes, then gently reshape with a toothpick.

Tracing paper makes an excellent nonstick material for wrapping ornaments for storage. Allow painted ornaments to cure for seven days before packing.

Applying Leading

1. Poke hole in tip of liquid leading bottle using a large paper clip.

2. Holding bottle vertically and applying firm, even pressure, go over pattern outlines, making two sets of leaves. *Note: For optimal control, grasp bottle as if you were holding a broomstick.* Keeping bottle tip above work, allow an even "rope" of leading to fall in place over pattern lines. To end a line, gently touch tip to glass and release pressure on bottle at the same time.

3. Set aside leading to dry completely before filling in with window colors—about 24 hours, depending on heat and humidity.

Applying Colors

1. First squeeze a line of color along inside of leaded outlines; this prevents color from shrinking away from outline as it dries.

2. Using even pressure, fill remaining areas with a generous amount of window color by moving the tip back and forth, as if coloring a picture.

3. Tap underside of project to raise most of the bubbles to the top, then gently comb through colored areas with a toothpick, popping bubbles as necessary. *Note: It helps to keep the end of the toothpick very dry.*

4. Set aside painted designs to dry completely—about 24 hours, depending on heat and humidity. Colors are

Old-fashioned glass tree ornaments are more popular than ever! Make your own stunning examples with plain ornaments and dazzling glass paints.

translucent and no longer cloudy when dry.

Poinsettia Ornament

1. Place picture-frame glass over patterns and outline each of the poinsettias with gold glitter leading; let dry undisturbed for at least eight hours.

2. Fill in entire outline of poinsettias with a thick coat of ruby red; allow window color to dry overnight.

3. Carefully peel off painted.poinsettias and arrange as desired on glass ornament, pressing into place. Place a gemstone in the center of each poinsettia and press. Squeeze a line of gold glitter leading around each gemstone and let dry.

4. Fill in entire background of ornament (around poinsettias) with crystal clear window color, using a circular motion. Hang ornament to dry and cure.

Candy Stripe Ornament

1. Make four long, straight lines of silver glitter leading lengthwise across glass from picture frame; let dry overnight.

2. Gently peel off two of the leading lines from glass. Beginning at top of ornament, press leading line around ornament in a spiral pattern. Using a craft knife, carefully trim off the end of the piece and the beginning of a second piece; join ends

together smoothly on ornament and continue spiral until it ends at center bottom of ornament. Trim off excess.

3. Apply the end of the third piece of leading at same point where you began the first, then gradually adjust position of leading to create a stripe 1" wide; continue wrapping leading around ornament until it too ends at center bottom of ornament.

4. Fill in stripe with kelly green; hang to dry overnight.

5. Fill in remainder of ornament with white pearl window color, using a circular motion. Hang ornament to dry and cure.

Starburst Ornament

1. Remove hanger loop and cap from ornament; stand ornament in cup, with opening facing up. Beginning at top and using gold glitter leading, squeeze a series of lines of varying lengths in a star pattern around opening. Use a toothpick to feather through lines from top down; this will thin lines out and give a more natural appearance. Let dry overnight.

2. Turn ornament over and repeat step 1, using bottom center of ornament as starting point. Press gemstone into center bottom of gold starburst. Let dry overnight

3. Replace hanging loop and cap on ornament. Fill in entire background with white pearl, using long vertical strokes. Hang ornament to dry and cure. ✿

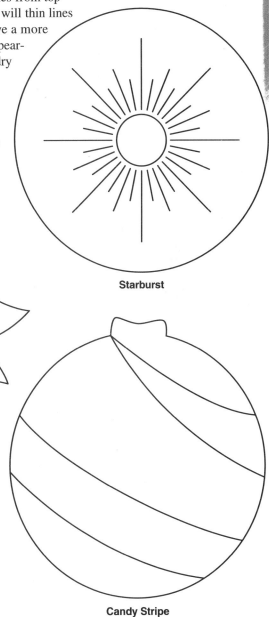

Starburst

Poinsettias

Candy Stripe

Angel Bears

Designs by Vicki Schreiner

Materials

- 10" x 20" piece ¼"-thick birch wood
- 18" ⅛"-wide metallic gold ribbon
- 3 jewelry screw eyes #5475 from Westrim
- Quick 'n Tacky adhesive from Delta
- Ceramcoat products from Delta: Faux Finish Glaze Base, Satin Exterior/Interior Water Based Varnish, Sparkle Glaze
- Ceramcoat acrylic paints from Delta: maple sugar tan #2062, brown velvet #2109, nightfall blue #2131, dusty mauve #2405, Bridgeport grey #2440, barn red #2490, white #2505, dark foliage green #2535
- Burnt umber oil color pencil from Walnut Hollow
- Creative Woodburner #5567 with Mini Flow Point #5593 and Shading Point #5594 from Walnut Hollow
- Paintbrushes: #4 and #6 flats, #3 round, #1 liner
- Graphite transfer paper
- Craft saw
- Fine-grit sandpaper
- Tack cloth
- Ballpoint pen
- Needle-nose pliers
- Toothpick
- Large-eye needle

Project Notes

Refer to photo and patterns throughout.

See directions for transferring pattern under "Using Transfer & Graphite Paper" in the General Instructions on page 190.

Follow manufacturer's instructions for using woodburning tool, heeding safety precautions.

Change tip to mini flow point and tighten with needle-nose pliers.

Before woodburning project, practice on a piece of scrap wood. Hold tool like a pen and use slow, short, sketching strokes to try straight and curved lines. Using a tapping motion, try making clusters of stippled dots (for fur).

To maintain even heat flow, occasionally clean tool by dragging the tip across sandpaper.

Mix equal parts paint and glaze base for all painting steps to create sheer color that will not hide the woodburning.

See directions for base-coating and shading under "Painting Techniques" in the General Instructions on page 191.

Let all coats of paints, glaze, varnish, etc., dry between applications.

Woodburning

1. Transfer outlines for three wings and one of each bear to wood; cut with saw. Sand until smooth; wipe off dust with tack cloth.

2. Transfer details of wings and bears to wooden pieces using graphite transfer paper and ballpoint pen.

3. Using mini flow point, woodburn outline of all designs except plaid on wings. Woodburn fur on head, arms and boy's feet using clusters of stippled dots. Make dots darker and denser in areas to be shaded, such as outside of head, around snout, tops and bases of ears, and outer edges of arms.

4. Darkly fill in inner ears and noses.

5. Change tip to shading point; tighten with needle-nose pliers. Using flat side of point, darkly fill outer flat edges (cut edges) around all pieces.

Painting & Detailing

1. Base-coat all wings with maple sugar tan; shade with brown velvet; line with dark foliage green and barn red.

2. Base-coat aprons with white; shade with Bridgeport grey.

3. Base-coat praying girl's dress with dark forest green; shade with additional dark foliage green. Base-coat cuffs and waistband with barn red; shade with additional barn red. Base-coat flowers on apron with barn red; add dark foliage green leaves. Using toothpick dipped in white, add tiny dot to center of each flower.

4. Base-coat remaining girl's dress with barn red; shade with additional barn red. Base-coat cuffs and waistband with dark foliage green; shade with additional dark foliage green. Base-coat hearts on apron with barn red; add dark foliage green leaves. Using toothpick dipped in white, add tiny dots to bear's eyes.

5. Base-coat boy's overalls with nightfall blue; shade with additional nightfall blue. Base-coat patch and shirt with barn red; shade shirt with additional barn red. Line stripes onto shirt with foliage green.

6. Clean paint from wood-burned grooves using very sharp oil color pencil.

7. *Cheeks:* Load brush with a small amount of dusty mauve paint; stroke off excess onto paper towel until dry, then stipple dry brush onto cheeks.

8. Glue wings on backs of bodies. Apply one coat sparkle glaze to front of

Who could resist these angelic little teddy bears? Cut the simple shapes from wood, then paint and add woodburned details for delightful results.

each wing and to hearts and flowers on aprons. Apply one coat of satin varnish to fronts of all bears and wings.

9. Using needle, push small hole into center top edge of each head. Place a small dot of adhesive in each hole and screw in eye screw. Cut ribbon into three 6" pieces; thread each piece through eye screw and knot ends for hanging loop. ❀

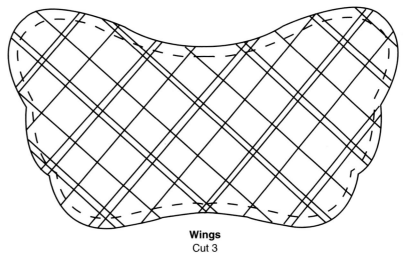

Wings
Cut 3

Patterns continued on page 189

Bake 'n' Shrink Pin

Designs by Samantha McNesby

Materials

- Sharpie medium-point black permanent marker
- Small paintbrush
- ¼" round hole punch
- 1 sheet Shrink-It Opake shrink plastic from Aleene's
- Black ballpoint pen
- Acrylic paints: red, green, blue, metallic gold
- 3 (8mm) gold jump rings
- 1 pin back
- Needle-nose pliers
- Thick craft glue or hot-glue gun

Project Notes

Refer to photo and patterns throughout.

Refer to manufacturer's instructions for using and shrinking plastic.

Apply very light coats of paint; colors will darken considerably when baked.

Instructions

1. Using marker, trace three small tree lights and the outline of one Merry Christmas panel onto shrink plastic, leaving at least ¾" between drawings. Add "Merry Christmas" to panel with marker.

2. Using ballpoint pen, trace strands of lights onto panel.

3. Paint all light sockets on tree lights, including tiny lights on panel, with metallic gold. Paint tiny lights on panel red, green and blue as desired. Paint one small tree light blue, one green and one red, leaving the highlight area unpainted.

4. Let paints dry completely, then cut out ¼" beyond outlines. Punch holes in panel and small tree lights with hole punch where indicated.

5. Bake pieces according to manufacturer's instructions. Let plastic cool completely before handling.

6. Attach small tree lights to panel with jump rings and needle-nose pliers. Glue pin back to back of panel; allow glue to cure 24 hours before wearing. ❀

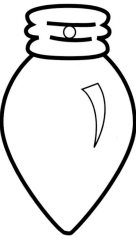

Small Tree Light
Cut 3

Shrinking plastic is the perfect material for creating fun holiday jewelry that can be used next year as tree trims.

Merry Christmas Pin
Cut 1

Angel Bears continued from page 187

Girl Bear

Praying Girl Bear

Boy Bear

General Instructions

Materials

In addition to the materials listed for each craft, some of the following crafting supplies may be needed to complete your projects. No doubt most of these are already on hand in your "treasure chest" of crafting aids. If not, you may want to gather them before you begin working so that you'll be able to complete each design quickly and without a hitch!

General Crafts

- Scissors
- Pencil
- Ruler
- Tracing paper
- Craft knife
- Heavy-duty craft cutters or wire nippers
- Plenty of newspapers to protect work surface

Painted Items

- Paper towels
- Paper or plastic foam plate or tray to use as a disposable paint palette for holding and mixing paints
- Plastic—a garbage bag, grocery sack, etc.—to protect your work surface
- Container of water or other recommended cleaning fluid for rinsing and cleaning brushes

Fabric Projects

- Iron and ironing board
- Pressing cloth
- Basic sewing notions
- Rotary cutter and self-healing mat
- Air-soluble markers
- Tailor's chalk

Reproducing Patterns & Templates

The patterns provided in this book are shown right side up, as they should look on the finished project; a few oversize patterns that need to be enlarged are clearly marked. Photocopiers with enlarging capabilities are readily available at copy stores and office supply stores. Simply copy the page, setting the photocopier to enlarge the pattern to the percentage indicated.

Patterns that do not need to be enlarged may be reproduced simply by placing a piece of tracing paper or vellum over the pattern in the book, and tracing the outlines carefully with a pencil or other marker.

Once you've copied your pattern pieces, cut them out and use these pieces as templates to trace around. Secure them as needed with pins or pattern weights.

If you plan to reuse the patterns or if the patterns are more intricate, with sharp points, etc., make sturdier templates by gluing the copied page of patterns onto heavy cardboard or template plastic. Let the glue dry, then cut out the pieces with a craft knife.

Depending on the application, it may be preferable to trace the patterns onto the wrong side of the fabric or other material so that no lines will be visible from the front. In this case, make sure you place the right side of the pattern piece against the wrong side of the fabric, paper or other material so that the piece will face the right direction when it is cut out.

Using Transfer & Graphite Paper

Some projects recommend transferring patterns to wood or another material with transfer or graphite paper. Read the manufacturer's instructions before beginning.

Lay tracing paper over the printed pattern and trace it carefully. Then place transfer paper transfer side down on wood or other material to be marked. Lay traced pattern on top. Secure layers with low-tack masking tape or tacks to keep pattern and transfer paper from shifting while you work.

Using a stylus, pen or other marking implement, retrace the pattern lines using smooth, even pressure to transfer the design onto surface.

Painted Designs

Disposable paper or plastic foam plates, including supermarket meat trays, make good palettes for pouring and mixing paints.

The success of a painted project often depends a great deal on the care taken in the initial preparations, including sanding,

applying primer and/or applying a base coat of color. Follow instructions carefully in this regard.

Take special care when painting sections adjacent to each other with different colors; allow the first color to dry so that the second will not run or mix. When adding designs atop a painted base, let the base coat dry thoroughly first.

If you will be mixing media, such as drawing with marking pens on a painted surface, test the process and your materials on scraps to make sure there will be no unsightly running or bleeding.

Keep your work surface and your tools clean. Clean brushes promptly in the manner recommended by the paint manufacturer; many acrylics can be cleaned up with soap and water, while other paints may require a solvent of some kind. Suspend your paintbrushes by their handles to dry so that the fluid drains out completely without bending the bristles.

Work in a well-ventilated area when using paints, solvents or finishes that emit fumes; read product labels thoroughly to be aware of any potential hazards and precautions.

Painting Techniques

Base-coating: Load paintbrush evenly with color by dabbing it on paint can lid, then coat surfaces with one or two smooth, solid coats of paint, letting paint dry between coats.

Dry-brushing: Dip a dry round-bristle brush in paint; wipe excess paint off onto paper towel until brush is almost dry. Wipe brush across edges for subtle shading.

Floating: Dampen brush with water. Touch one side of brush into paint, then sweep brush back and forth on palette to work paint into the brush. Apply the color around the edges of the area you are working on as directed in your painting instructions.

Rouging: Dip dry, round bristle brush in paint and wipe paint off onto paper towel until brush is almost completely dry and leaves no visible brush strokes. Wipe brush across area to be rouged using a circular motion.

Shading: Dip angled shader brush in water and blot lightly once on paper towel, leaving some water in brush. Dip point of brush into paint. Stroke onto palette once or twice to blend paint into water on bristles so that stroke has paint on one side gradually blending to no color on the other side.

Highlighting: Wet flat brush with water; dry on paper towel. Dip corner of brush into paint and brush back and forth on palette until color goes from dark value to light.

Stenciling: Dip dry stencil brush in paint. Wipe brush on paper towel, removing excess paint to prevent seepage under stencil. Brush cutout areas with a circular motion, holding brush perpendicular to surface. When shading, the brush should be almost dry, working only around edges. Use masking tape to hold stencil in place while working.

Buyer's Guide

Projects in this book were made using products provided by the manufacturers listed below. Look for the suggested products in your local craft- and art-supply stores. If unavailable, contact suppliers below. Some may be able to sell products directly to you; others may be able to refer you to retail sources.

Aleene's
Div. of Duncan Enterprises
5673 E. Shields Ave.
Fresno, CA 93727
(800) 237-2642;
www.duncan-enterprises.com

All Night Media
Div. of Plaid Enterprises
3225 Westech Dr.
Norcross, GA 30092
(800) STAMPED;
www.allnightmedia.com

ArtEmboss
American Art Clay Co. Inc.
4717 W. 16th St.
Indianapolis, IN 46222-2598
(317) 244-6871
www.amaco.com

Beacon Adhesives/
Signature Marketing
P.O. Box 427
Wyckoff, NJ 07481
(800) 865-7238;
www.beacon1.com

Bemiss-Jason
525 Enterprise
Neenah, WI 54957
(800) 544-0093;
www.bemiss-jason.com

Clearsnap Inc.
Box 98
Anacortes, WA 98221
(360) 293-6634;
www.clearsnap.com

Craft Stamp
P.O. Box 681
Oak Lawn, IL 60454
(773) 585-6918

Craftware
629 Boyette Rd.
Four Oak, NC 27524
(800) 927-7714;
www.craft-ware.com

C-Thru Ruler Co.
Déjà Views
6 Britton Dr.
Bloomfield, CT 06002-3602
(800) 243-8419
www.cthruruler.com

Darice Inc.
Mail-order source: **Bolek's**
330 N. Tuscarawas Ave.
Dover, OH 44622
(330) 364-8878

DecoArt
P.O. Box 386
Stanford, KY 40484
(800) 367-3047; www.decoart.com

Delta Technical Coatings
2550 Pellissier Pl.
Whittier, CA 90601-1505
(800) 423-4135;
www.deltacrafts.com

EK Success Ltd.
125 Entin Rd.
Clifton, NJ 07014
(800) 524-1349;
www.eksuccess.com

EtchAll/
B & B Etching Products Inc.
19721 N. 98th Ave.
Peoria, AZ 85382
(888) 382-4255; www.etchall.com

Fibre-Craft Materials Corp.
Mail-order source: **Kirchen Brothers**
P.O. Box 1016
Skokie, IL 60076
(800) 378-5024;
e-mail: kirchenbro@aol.com

Fiskars Inc.
7811 W. Stewart Ave.
Wausau, WI 54401
(800) 950-0203, Ext. 1277;
www.fiskars.com

Forster Inc./
Diamond Brands
1800 Cloquet Ave.
Cloquet, MN 55720
(218) 879-6700;
www.diamondbrands.com/forster.html

Halcraft USA
30 W. 24th St.
New York, NY 10010-3207
(212) 376-1580; www.halcraft.com

IKEA
496 W. Germantown Pike
Plymouth Meeting, PA 19462
(703) 494-4532;
www.ikea-usa.com

James Button & Trim
615 N. New St.
Allentown, PA 18012
(610) 865-9530

Krylon/Sherwin-Williams Co.
Craft Customer Service
101 Prospect Ave. N.W.
Cleveland, OH 44115
(800) 247-3268;
www.krylon.com

Kunin Felt Co./Foss Mfg. Co. Inc.
P.O. Box 5000
Hampton, NH 03842-5000
(603) 929-6100;
www.kuninfelt.com

Lara's Crafts
590 N. Beach St.
Fort Worth, TX 76111
(800) 232-5272;
www.larascrafts.com

Marvy/Uchida of America Corp.
3535 Del Amo Blvd.
Torrance, CA 90503
(800) 541-5877; www.uchida.com

Micron/Sakura of America
30780 San Clemente St.
Hayward, CA 94544
(800) 776-6257; www.gellyroll.com

Nature's Pressed
P.O. Box 212
Orem, UT 84059
(800) 850-2499;
www.naturespressed.com

Paper Reflections/
DMD Industries Inc.
1250 ESI Dr.
Springdale, AR 72764
(800) 805-9890; www.dmdind.com

Pebeo of America Inc.
P.O. Box 717
Swanton, VT 05488
(819) 829-5012; www.pebeo.com

Pellon Consumer Products
3440 Industrial Dr.
Durham, NC 27704
(919) 620-3916

Personal Stamp Exchange
360 Sutton Pl.
Santa Rosa, CA 95407
(800) 782-6748;
www.psxstamps.com

Plaid Enterprises Inc.
3225 Westech Dr.
Norcross, GA 30092
(800) 842-4197;
www.plaidonline.com

Polyform Products Co.
1901 Estes Ave.
Elk Grove Village, IL 60007
(847) 427-0020; www.sculpey.com

Pop-Up Paper Room Accessories/
Beckhill Group Ltd.
175 Bryant Ave.
Glen Ellyn, IL 60137
www.popuppaper.com

Provo Craft
Mail-order source: **Creative Express**
295 W. Center St.
Provo, UT 84601-4436
(800) 563-8679;
www.creativeexpress.com

Rubber Stampede Inc.
P.O. Box 246
Berkeley, CA 94701
(800) 632-8386;
www.rstampede.com

Sculpey III/
Polyform Products Co.
1901 Estes Ave.
Elk Grove Village, IL 60007
(847) 427-0020; www.sculpey.com

Seaside Crafter's Edition
Distributed nationwide by
JoAnn Stores

Therm O Web
770 Glenn Ave.
Wheeling, IL 60090
(847) 520-5200;
www.thermoweb.com

Tsukineko
15411 NE 95th St.
Redmond, WA 98052
(800) 769-6633;
www.tsukineko.com

Tulip Div. of Duncan Enterprises
5673 E. Shields Ave.
Fresno, CA 93727
(800) 237-2642;
www.duncan-enterprises.com

V.I.P. Fabrics
1412 Broadway
New York, NY 10018
(800) 847-4064

Walnut Hollow Farms Inc.
1409 State Rd. 23
Dodgeville, WI 53533-2112
(800) 950-5101;
www.walnuthollow.com

Warm & Natural/The Warm Co.
954 E. Union St.
Seattle, WA 98122
(800) 234-WARM;
www.warmcompany.com

Westrim Crafts/
Western Trimming Corp.
9667 Canoga
Chatsworth, CA 91311
(818) 998-8550

Wild Wire/
Natural Science Industries Ltd.
910 Orlando Ave.
West Hempstead, NY 11552-3942
(516) 678-1700;
www.wild-wire.com

Wimpole Street Creations
Mail-order source: **Barrett House**
P.O. Box 540585
North Salt Lake, UT 84054-0585
(801) 299-0700;
e-mail: wimpole@xmission.com